The Road to Grace

Finding True Freedom from the Bondage of Sexual Addiction

MIKE GENUNG

Blazing Grace Publishing ✦ Colorado Springs, CO

BLAZING GRACE PUBLISHING
PO Box 25763
Colorado Springs, CO 80936

The Road to Grace; Finding True Freedom
from the Bondage of Sexual Addiction

©2006–2014 by Mike Genung

Scripture quotations taken from the New American Standard Bible®, Copyright ©1960, 1962, 1963, 1968, 1971, 1972, 1973, 1975, 1977, 1995 by The Lockman Foundation. Used by permission. www.Lockman.org

The stories that appear in this book are based on the lives of real people. Names and details have been changed to protect the confidentiality of these individuals.

Cover Design ©2006 TLC Graphics, www.TLCGraphics.com.

ISBN-13: 978-0-9787756-0-5
ISBN-10: 0-9787756-0-0

SAN: 851-6022

Printed in USA

More copies of this book can be ordered at *www.roadtograce.net*.

To Michelle

*You unknowingly married a young man in 1989 who
was a sex addict, and then endured 10 years of sorrow as he
was unfaithful to you mentally, physically and emotionally.
The grace you have shown by forgiving me for
wounding you so deeply is priceless.*

You are my soul mate, and I love you.

To Jesus

*This book was written because You changed my life
by filling my heart with the love of God, in spite of the fact
that I'd spent much of my life betraying You. Thank You
for bringing this prodigal son home. You are my
First Love. May You use this book to set the hearts
of many on fire with love for You.*

Table of Contents

~~~

chapter one

Lies, Truth, and Hope

⌒

BUT WE SHOULD ALWAYS GIVE THANKS TO GOD FOR YOU,
BRETHREN BELOVED BY THE LORD, BECAUSE GOD HAS CHOSEN YOU
FROM THE BEGINNING FOR SALVATION THROUGH SANCTIFICATION
BY THE SPIRIT AND FAITH IN THE TRUTH.

2 Thessalonians 2:13

I realized I had a serious problem with sexual addiction in June of 1991. I was out of control, masturbating with pornography at least once a day. It didn't matter if I was home alone when my wife, Michelle, was out of the house, or if I was in a hotel room when traveling for business.

I fell hardest in the hotels. The isolation and loneliness, coupled with the temptation to watch a porn movie, were too much for me. I'd spend the night binging on lust, and would face a long day of sales calls on two hours of sleep and a raging hangover of shame.

I'd attended church most of my life and knew all of the "sexually immoral shall not inherit the kingdom of God" verses, but the fear of judgment did little more than add to my burden of shame. Willpower didn't work; I tried to quit many times. The harder I fought the more I fell. Like most naïve young men, I thought getting married would eliminate my lust problem, but the inevitable friction that surfaces between a man and woman raised in completely different, often dysfunctional family settings had me running to porn more than when I was single. My innocent young wife of two years knew the Christian Dr. Jekyll side of me, but she didn't know about the guy hiding in the shadows, Mr. Hyde.

Since other Christians didn't talk about struggling with porn or sexual sin, I assumed something was seriously wrong with *me*; I even had doubts if I was really a Christian. I figured I better get help before I went too far and lost my marriage.

But… where should I go for help?

I knew I couldn't go to the church; I'd tried *that* before. In 1990, Michelle and I went to a church-sponsored marriage retreat in the San Bernardino Mountains. Unbeknownst to my wife, I'd gone on a porn binge a few days before the retreat and, as usual, was hung over from shame.

We warmed up on Saturday morning by singing praises to God. The clean, uplifting music and the sights of God's majestic creation rubbed salt in my sores of shame. As the morning progressed it got worse until I couldn't take it any longer; I had to talk to someone. The retired pastor who was teaching seemed warm and friendly, and I decided to talk to him about my struggle with porn.

When we were dismissed for the break, I told Michelle I wanted to talk to the retreat leader for a moment and would catch up with her later. I approached him nervously; I'd never opened up to anyone with this before…

"Hi uhh, I appreciate the things you're sharing with us… and I… uh… I'm having a problem with something I need to talk about."

He smiled: "Sure! What's the problem?"

I felt a bit of relief wash over me. So far this was going well. "I... uh... have a problem..." I swallowed hard. "With pornography... it's something I've struggled with for a long time... I was hoping you might have some advice for what to do...."

His expression darkened; he was obviously in the presence of a sinner, me, and I needed to be set straight. He bored into me with his eyes and let loose: "Just stop doing it! Just stop!"

I nodded weakly and walked away, looking for a hole to crawl into, thankful the retreat leader didn't attend my church.

I shuddered. What if I'd told someone from my church? I could see the announcement in the Sunday morning bulletin now: "Mike Genung confessed he's a sex addict; First Corinthians expulsion ceremony tonight at 6:30 p.m. in the worship center; coffee and dessert will be served afterwards."

I'd been going to a female Christian psychologist for a few years, but I couldn't talk to a woman about my porn problem. I thought about my male friends, but all the men I spent time with worked in the same industry I did; if they spread the word that "Mike's a porno"... I didn't want to think about it.

What about my wife? Oh yeah, I could see it now. "Honey, I can't stop masturbating to pictures of other naked women... think you can pray for me?" I'd be singing the country song that lady who'd been married seven times used to sing: "D–I–V–O–R–C–E." All our friends would know and I'd have to move to some desolate place like Alaska to start over.

My church, my counselor, my friends and my wife were out. What was left?

I'd heard about Alcoholics Anonymous and thought perhaps there was a similar program for people who struggled with sexual addiction. I looked in the yellow pages and found a 12-step group for sex addicts. The meetings were held once a week in a city 45 minutes away by car, and they met that night.

I mumbled to Michelle about having something I needed to take care of, and took off on the 60 freeway heading east. Normally I would have enjoyed the drive, but I was too nervous about the meeting. I pictured myself sitting in a dimly lit room with a bunch of sleazy-looking guys wearing dirty clothes and mean expressions. I almost turned back.

The meeting was held in a mental hospital consisting of flat, white buildings, with a look not unlike an insane asylum. I entered the front building and approached the visitor station, which was attended by a girl dressed in street clothes. A wave of shame surged over me; telling a woman that I struggled with lust was the last thing I wanted to do.

"Where's the room for… uh… the group for sex addiction?" She looked at me as if I was just another mental case and pointed me to where I needed to go, a room around the corner from her station.

I took a deep breath and walked in. The carpeted room was a long rectangle in shape, 25 feet long and 10 feet wide, with contemporary art decorating the clean white walls. A long wood conference table filled the room, and, seated in the plush office chairs were eight men; not one of whom looked like I'd imagined they would. A few were dressed in suits, and the rest wore clean, casual clothes.

The meeting began with everyone introducing themselves and discussing a little of their background. With each new introduction, my eyes widened and my jaw dropped a little more. *Almost all of them were Christians.* They weren't just pew warmers either. One guy had been a senior pastor and another, a music minister. Their struggles were similar to mine; all of them had a problem with porn and masturbation, while some added promiscuity, affairs, and prostitution to the mix.

"*What's going on here?*" I thought. "This is a secular program, yet most of the guys here are Christians. Could it be there are more in the church who have a problem with sexual sin than I imagined?"

Since that night, I've attended and led many meetings for the sexually broken; I've seen pastors, priests, music ministers, elders, and missionaries at these groups. Pornography and sexual sin have infiltrated the church at every level, and yet the subject is rarely discussed, especially from the pulpit. I think most people still see pornography as I once did: a problem on the fringes of society, something a few dirty old men go to grimy adult bookstores in the industrial part of town to buy.

Today the grim reality is that porn is as American as apple pie, and many Christians are feasting on it. Take a look at these statistics:

+ The revenues of the porn industry in the U.S are approximately 13 billion; equivalent to the annual revenues of the NFL and NBA combined.[1]

+ 30 % of all internet traffic is pornography; the world's largest porn site alone transfers 29 *petabytes* of porn a month.[2]

+ 67 % of men and 49 % of women say porn is acceptable.[3]

+ In the UK, porn websites are accessed more than social media or shopping sites.[4]

+ One Christian missions agency is reported as saying that 80 % of their applicants admit to struggles with porn. They know longer ask "if" but "how often."[5]

+ A survey of 19,000 parents revealed that kids are viewing porn as early as age six.[6]

+ A London survey of 800 young people showed that most teenage boys view porn 2-3 times per week, on their phone or bedroom computer. 2/3 of those between 11 and 13 had viewed it.[7]

+ One youth minister states that 90 % of the kids who come to him for help, all from Christian families, are addicted to porn.[8]

+ 21 % of Christian teenage girls admit to texting a naked photo of themselves.[9]

+ 50 % of pastors regularly view porn.[10]

+ 56 % of divorce cases involve one person with problems with pornography.[11]

I know the statistics are overwhelming and shocking; the idea that *at least* half of Christian men could have a problem with porn is hard to grasp. Sunday morning at church you look at the faces in the crowd, many of whom you know, and think, "It can't be… not in *my* church."

I had thought the same thing. In early 2004, the pastor at the church where I attended agreed to let me survey the men on the subject of pornography. Our body of 600 was mainly families, and I couldn't imagine so many Christian fathers and husbands I sat next to every Sunday indulging in porn. To my surprise the results mirrored the national surveys: 25 % of the men who responded had viewed porn within the past month; 44 % within the past six months, and 61 % within the past year.

But if you look only at the numbers, it's easy to forget there are real people with—oftentimes—tragic stories to tell behind the statistics:

+ Tom is a one-time church elder, married to a woman who'd been a missionary before they were married. They have three children, and have served together in the children's ministry at their church. Tom's addiction to porn and masturbation brought their marriage to a crisis point when his wife walked in on him as he was masturbating with pornographic magazines.

✦ Sammy was a married father of two children; he served as the music minister in his church with his wife, who sang in the choir. Both Sammy and his wife had a problem with lust; Sammy struggled with porn and masturbation while his wife had adulterous affairs. Their divorce had a profound effect on their teenage daughter, who ended up in a mental hospital on suicide watch.

✦ Jim is a Christian who has struggled with porn, masturbation, and promiscuity. While married to his second wife, Jim had sex with a prostitute. Overcome with guilt, he went to his church and confessed his sin to the leaders of his church, who then anointed him with oil and prayed over him. Jim felt better after he left, but then the loneliness that plagued him all of his life hit with full force, and he went to a second prostitute that same night. His wife filed for divorce a few months later.

✦ Bill was a married father of two who'd struggled with porn and masturbation for most of his life. He'd spent many years in various 12-step and other recovery programs, and had led a support group at his church. Bill had moved away from porn but couldn't give up masturbation; he didn't see anything wrong with it, even though his wife begged him to change. He told me his wife would watch him go into their bedroom alone, knowing he was going to have sex with himself. Over a three-year period their marriage slowly died. In that time there was not even one moment of physical intimacy between them. Several months later, Bill's wife filed for divorce.

✦ Marcus was a respected law enforcement officer who was married to a woman with a teenage daughter from a previous marriage; he also had a secret problem with porn and masturbation. One night, Marcus allowed his lust to take him to his stepdaughter's bedroom, with devastating consequences. He lost his family, his job, and his freedom. Marcus served five years in prison.

✦ Jeff got into the homosexual lifestyle as a teenager, then found the Lord in his early twenties. Determined to live for Christ, he made a clean break from his sinful past and got involved with a church; after a few years the Lord provided him with a strong Christian woman for a wife. Life was going well, but then his wife was killed in a tragic car accident. Overwhelmed with grief and sudden isolation, Jeff started slipping back into homosexual pornography and masturbation.

✦ Rich is a Christian who's married to a beautiful, intelligent woman with whom he has three kids. He and his wife are blessed financially; together they make 250,000 dollars a year. They have a million dollar home, new cars, and all the toys. In spite of spending 14 years in the 12-step program for sexual addiction, in the past two years Rich's struggle with porn and masturbation has gone from ugly to out of control. Rich is one of my closest friends, and I'm praying his addiction to sexual sin doesn't take another family out.

When men walk into our support group the first time I often hear them say, "I thought I was the only Christian who had a problem with lust." Satan's strategy is to convince the struggler with sexual sin that he must keep it a secret. If I'm "the only one" then I dare not tell others because I don't want to be at the wrong end of a witch hunt. No one can understand my problem which means there is no hope, so I can never be freed from the shame and sin that so easily take me down. The result is that despair and sexual idolatry reign in my life.

When we keep lust a secret, it rules over us. For years, I let lies and accusations like these keep me from seeking help:

"You can't tell anyone."

"What will they think of you if they know what you're doing?"

"You're a *Christian* and you're doing this?!"

"No one else has this problem so you must be a freak, or a pervert...."

"You'll get kicked out of the church if you tell someone there... aren't you ashamed of yourself?!"

And then, worst of all, "You've already sinned so you might as well take the next step... Hey, it's just a little porn; you're alone now and no one else is watching; what will it hurt?"

Satan's intent is to keep you trapped in sin and shame, but Almighty God's plan is to set you free. I've seen Him change the lives of the sexually broken, including men who've ended up in prison, and then use them to minister to others. I've seen marriages saved from divorce, and I've seen men who masturbated every day for years stop. He's changed the lives of many who've struggled with sexual sin, including my own, and He's willing, ready, and waiting to do the same for you, no matter what you've done. I believe the fact that you're reading this book shows He's working in your life and drawing you to Him.

You're not the only Christian who struggles with lust; you're not a one-of-a-kind pervert, and there is abundant hope. If you'll let Him, the Lord will change your life. Let's strike out on the road to grace together; the journey may be rough at times, but the end result will be more than worth it.

chapter two

Isolation
is Death

HE WHO ISOLATES HIMSELF SEEKS HIS OWN DESIRE;
HE QUARRELS AGAINST ALL SOUND WISDOM.

Proverbs 18:1

We men are drawn to stories of valiant, courageous war-
riors. We picture ourselves as Braveheart, leading a
rough 'n rowdy group of guys against an evil empire and wip-
ing them out; Rocky, winning the boxing title in the last
minute of a ferocious battle; or the superhero of our choice
who overcomes the villain and saves the day.

Some of us might aspire to be a heroic man of God, like
Elijah, a man of strong faith who took on the nation of Israel
and saw God come through powerfully, or Stephen, who put
his life on the line and faced the Pharisees, or Paul, a bold witness of the gospel in the midst of fierce opposition, beatings,
and tribulations. We love tales of bravery and all-out risk
because we want to be the kind of man who lives life this way.

A guy who can admit his weaknesses and faults is a man
with guts. It takes courage and a passionate commitment to

Christ to ignore our pride and confess that our lives are a mess. When another man is brutally honest with his weaknesses, he inspires and challenges others to want to be like him. True strength is measured in a man's heart, not his bench press.

A few years back, a guy who struggled with porn came to our Strength in Numbers group for the first time. He was 6'3", of strong build, had a beard, and had been in the military. From the outside, this guy was a man's man. He arrived 10 minutes early, and while we waited for the others to arrive he asked some questions about the meeting.

"How many guys come to this group?" he asked. At the time, we were averaging five guys a night; joking, I said "Oh, about 25." His knees literally buckled; he looked at me with terror and said "I'm outta here!" The idea of having to tell a large group of men that he struggled with porn and masturbation was too much for him. I quickly calmed him down, assuring him that we wouldn't have 25 men that night.

To admit a struggle with porn, masturbation, or some other sexual sin can be a terrifying prospect. Shame, fear of rejection, and the threat to pride are real enemies that must be faced. There is a risk that the person we tell could dress us down or reject us, like the retired pastor did to me as I shared in chapter one. But, although some in the body of Christ may be uncomfortable with our stinky laundry, there are many others who can relate—and will be blessed by our honesty. Remember, at least half of the men in the church have an issue with porn.

"Why should I tell another person about my struggle with sexual sin?" you ask. "Isn't there another way?"

In the battle against lust, willpower doesn't work; the fact that you're reading this book is probably proof of it. To defeat lust on our own we would have to be able to reach into our heart and clean it out; it would be like a man attempting to operate on himself for cancer.

Like every other man, I tried everything I could to avoid exposing my sexual sin to another. I made vows to God that I broke, prayed and read my Bible every day, memorized scripture, and fasted. I also made bold, heroic moves to try to conquer lust. One night while on a business trip alone in a hotel room, I cut the plug off the power cord to the TV with my pocket knife so I wouldn't watch it. However, once the waves of lust started rolling over me, I spliced the wires of the power cord and inserted them into the wall socket. Unfortunately, I crossed a hot wire with a neutral one and shorted out the entire circuit of my room. Too embarrassed to tell hotel management what had happened, I spent the rest of my stay in darkness.

So much for willpower.

In his book *Pure Desire*, Ted Roberts compares lust with a noose:

> *As I have spoken through the years to many groups on the topic of sexual struggles, again and again I encounter those who, unfortunately, have been given deadly advice. A spiritual leader has told them they simply need to read their Bibles more, pray more and try harder next time so they won't do it again.*

> *In such instances, the counselor was oblivious to the spiritual noose around the person's soul, a noose that tightened and made things worse the more the person pulled. What that person really needed was to cut the rope! Telling someone to pull harder isn't going to work. In fact, it's counterproductive![1]*

Lust feeds, breeds, and thrives off of isolation; the harder we fight against it, the stronger it gets. I have yet to hear of one person who's been able to kick lust on their own, and I've been around men and women who struggle with it since

1991. In this battle, isolation is death; the only way to take away lust's power is to eliminate the fuel that feeds it.

The American Heritage Dictionary defines the word isolate as "to set apart or cut off from others." Being alone is not the same as "setting apart from." You can be at peace in solitude by communing with God, listening to uplifting music, reading a book, or exercising. Jesus often spent time alone with God, so a solitary life is not necessarily an isolated one. We "cut ourselves off" from others, especially those who love us, when we turn inward and withdraw into our shell. I've spent years of my married life emotionally isolated, or "set apart" from my wife. You can be isolated in a crowd of people, just as you can be connected to God and others in solitude.

When a person is floundering in shame, the natural response is to "set apart from others" emotionally. This "setting apart from" has the insidious effect of giving lust what it needs to grow like a weed on steroids. A man who's cut off from love still has to feed on something emotionally, so he settles for the garbage of lust.

God's word speaks to the insanity of isolation, and what happens when we keep our sin hidden:

> *He who isolates himself seeks his own desire;*
> *he quarrels against all sound wisdom.*
>
> PROVERBS 18:1

> *When I kept silent about my sin, my body wasted*
> *away through my groaning all day long.*
>
> PSALMS 32:3

When one who's trapped on the merry-go-round of sexual addiction is in the hunt for a lust-fix, all that matters is "seeking his own desire." Life becomes "all about me," and all sound wisdom is thrown out the window. This is the insane, Jekyll and Hyde life of a Christian sex addict: they know

God's word and His commands against sexual sin, yet they "quarrel against it" and "seek their own desire."

When we "set apart" and hide our sin, we embrace it; embracing sin is worshipping it, and to worship sin is to become its slave. (*"For by what a man is overcome, by this he is enslaved,"* 2 Peter 2:19b.) A man who's "cut off from others" shoulders his heavy burden alone, and the daily grind from the oppression of sexual sin "wastes his body away." When sexual sin ruled my life I had trouble sleeping; I was often tired, and got sick easily. As time progressed I struggled with anxiety and panic attacks and was put on antidepressants; my nervous system was fried from the weight of my sin.

We can drop our load the easy way by sharing our struggles with others of our own free will, or we can do it the hard way and wait until "it" happens, like many men do. John was one of those who waited for "it." Addicted to porn for most of his life, John, a married man, decided to seek out a prostitute one night. Lust always leaves its victim wanting more, and pictures were no longer enough for John; he wanted the real thing. The prostitute he hit on was an undercover cop, and John's secret life was blown wide open, placing his marriage under immense strain. It was right after this that John contacted me for help.

What most guys don't realize is that sexual sin causes emotional and spiritual blindness. The former pastor at the church we attend used to say "sin makes you stupid." After spending years wandering in a dense fog of dimwittedness, I know he's right. Blind and self-absorbed, we can't see the oncoming semi truck until it's too late.

Would not God find this out?
For He knows the secrets of the heart.

PSALMS 44:21

If you won't expose your secret sexual sin, God will. In her book *An Affair of the Mind*, Laurie Hall recounts the following:

One day when Alice was cleaning her husband's hobby room, the Lord impressed on her that she needed to go look in the middle of a pile of old magazines. "What a ridiculous thought," she told herself. But it wouldn't go away. Finally, she walked over to the pile and pulled out the middle magazine. It was a copy of the latest edition of Playboy. Now the wadded-up, crisp towel she had found in Bob's underwear drawer when she was putting away his clean socks made sense. He'd been masturbating to pornography.

"I never would have believed he was into that stuff," she told me.

The Lord also opened Helen's eyes. Her husband, a deacon in the church, was extremely jealous and given to mood swings. One night, after Helen had been asking the Lord to reveal what was going on, the Lord woke her up and urged her to go to the family room.

"You've got to be kidding, Lord," she said, looking at the alarm clock. "It's 3:00 in the morning!" Then she became aware that Paul wasn't in bed. Walking into the family room, she was stunned to find her husband watching the Playboy channel."[2]

We can't hide our sin from the Lord; we can take the "easier road" and open up on our own, or let Him do it the hard and messy way. He loves you too much too allow you to continue in sin, and what you're doing is harmful to yourself and those who love you. I've heard stories from many men who had carefully covered their tracks by deleting the porn files on their computer, only to have their wife stumble on the one image they'd "somehow" forgotten.

The blowout from getting caught may be ugly, but God uses it to move a man or woman towards healing; He reveals His love for you even when He allows you to get caught. John later said that the day his sex addiction was exposed was a blessing from the Lord because he would have kept going otherwise.

He who conceals his transgressions will not prosper,
but he who confesses and forsakes them will find compassion.
PROVERBS 28:13

Therefore, confess your sins to one another, and pray for one
another so that you may be healed. The effective prayer
of a righteous man can accomplish much.
JAMES 5:16

Finding freedom from lust is impossible in isolation; those who conceal their sexual sin "will not prosper." To expose the wounds that keep you from receiving God's grace, we must stop the bleeding (sexual acting out), and the only way to stop acting out is to stay out of and away from isolation. There is no other way.

Staying out of isolation means we meet with one man or a group of guys at a support group on a consistent, weekly basis. A Christ-centered, grace-focused, support group that focuses on helping its members find true freedom from sexual sin is better than relying on one accountability partner. With a group, you have more support, encouragement, input and prayer in your behalf. At the Blazing Grace website (*www.blazinggrace.org*) we have information available on the location of our Strength in Numbers groups nationwide, or how you can start your own group.

Brethren, even if anyone is caught in any trespass, you who are
spiritual, restore such a one in a spirit of gentleness; each one
looking to yourself, so that you too will not be tempted.

GALATIANS 6:1

Many of the men who come to Strength in Numbers have few if any friends who they can share with; some are opening up for the first time in their lives. When a man walks into our group, he knows we know why he's there and there's no hiding; we get down to business and dispense with the small talk. In the process of unloading their burdens they discover that there's nothing like the blessing of having a group of guys who they can be honest with. Watching these men break free from shame and rediscover their strength is one of the greatest joys of my life.

We ask the guys to be honest with any lust of the mind, struggles with temptation, use of pornography, masturbation or sex outside of marriage. We require thorough honesty, not to embarrass or humiliate, but because hiding secrets keeps them trapped in shame. A guy who says "I acted out last night" will be asked for more details; an all-night porn binge in which a guy masturbated three times is different from glancing at a lingerie model on a news website for a few moments. To expel all of our shame, we must expose all of our secret sin.

How blessed is he whose transgression is forgiven, whose sin is covered! How blessed is the man to whom the Lord does not impute iniquity, and in whose spirit there is no deceit!

PSALMS 32:1–2

There is balance to what we reveal to others; be specific, but never graphic. Painting a picture of what you saw will draw those same images in the minds of your brothers and could trip them up. Keep it clean and avoid descriptive imagery. There's also no need to discuss details like the location of the adult bookstore you visited, or the URL of any porn websites.

When temptations hit during the week, get on the phone and bring another brother into the battle. Temptations that were towering giants vanish when exposed to the light of another. Resolve to stay out of isolation, and resist the temptation to take on Godzilla on your own. In chapter five we'll talk about how to deal with temptations in the mind.

Destroying isolation and shame takes an effective one-two punch. Read James 5:16 again:

> *Therefore, confess your sins to one another, and pray for one another so that you may be healed. The effective prayer of a righteous man can accomplish much.*

God promises that we will be healed after we confess our sins and our brothers pray for us; we jab with transparency, and then throw a right cross with the prayer of others. When others pray for our specific area of need, we allow the Spirit of God to speak, minister to, and heal us where we need it. This is why it's critical that we share *all* of our weaknesses, struggles, and temptations; our brothers can't pray for that which they're unaware of.

This doesn't mean that wham-bam, we pray, and slam dunk, all struggles with lust are gone. God's timing and ways aren't like ours, and He does thorough work. There may be times when He will flesh out other issues we need to see and deal with before He gets to what was prayed for. He hears every prayer and request, and knows the right process and timing for each individual.

I've seen God work miracles from prayer alone. Frank first came to our group not long after he'd exposed his affairs and struggle with porn and masturbation to his wife. She had kicked Frank out of the house and was demanding a divorce; to make matters worse her friends were poisoning her with the advice to "divorce the dirty blank-blank as soon as possible." They had two small kids, which meant that another family was about to be taken out by the black plague of sexual sin. To be honest, I had given up hope that their marriage would survive.

We continued to pray for Frank and his wife together at meetings and individually during the week, and God miraculously raised their marriage from the dead. God alone, working through the prayers of His people, saved Frank's marriage by softening his wife's heart. Frank did his part by staying out of isolation and away from lust; if he hadn't, Frank wouldn't have given his wife a reason to stay.

*Again I say to you, that if two of you agree on earth
about anything that they may ask, it shall be done for them
by My Father who is in heaven.*
MATTHEW 18:19

When Bill came to our group, his marriage was on the edge. He'd had multiple affairs a few years prior, and his wife had told Bill that she would never forgive him. Their marriage was a pressure cooker of stress and conflict. Week after week Bill came in with stories of fierce, angry battles; at one point she'd packed her suitcase and was ready to walk out the door. Although Bill had been going to groups and doing his part, his wife's heart was hardened in bitterness against him. We continued to pray, and God worked another miracle; Bill's wife forgave him and their marriage has been mending and growing ever since. The second part of James 5:16—"and pray for one another that you may be healed"—is just as critical as confessing our sins; any support group that neglects the power of prayer is missing out on a treasure trove of blessing.

The Lord commands us to confess our sins to each other and pray for each other because He wants to heal us, not shame or punish us. You'll never discover the incredible blessings of the James 5:16 way of life while hiding in isolation.

Should *you* tell your wife?

I could devote a chapter to answering this question; instead here are six reasons why those of us who are married should tell our wives of our struggle with porn or sexual sin:

+ The marriage is corrupted, and until you come clean the adulteress of lust will always be between you and your wife, thwarting intimacy, causing stress, and keeping you trapped in guilt and shame. Moreover, your porn addiction and deception are an open door of sin that Satan uses to corrupt you, your wife and your children. I've heard many stories over the years of men who got hooked on porn when they found their father's stash of magazines, and it's not uncommon to hear of a wife who looked at porn because she wanted to see what it was that entranced her husband. Recently, a wife posted the following on the forums of the Blazing Grace website:

About 6 months ago I had to go to the building out back where my husband keeps his bike and spends a lot of time to get some canning jars. I was looking for the lids and opened a cabinet to get some lids and there was a ton of porn magazines; I am not talking Playboy or a few naked girls. The hard part was that his 15-year-old daughter was standing there when I found them and she started to cry.

If you don't take action now, your wife could be posting something like this in our forums about your son or daughter. Please don't let it happen.

+ Your wife may not know what you've done, but she senses it and it will eat at her, sapping her desire for sexual intimacy and causing more friction in the marriage. Remember Helen's story? Her husband was "extremely jealous and given to mood swings." Of Alice's husband, Laurie Hall writes "her husband was distant emotionally and he had lost all sexual interest in her."[3] Sexual sin warps a man's character; your wife, who knows you better than anyone, can see it from a mile away. Once she starts seeking God for the truth, He can and will reveal it to her, just as He did with Helen and Alice.

✦ Many wives are far more angry and hurt from the lies and betrayal than by what their husband did. The American Heritage Dictionary defines betrayal as "To give aid or information to an enemy of… commit treason against… to deliver into the hands of an enemy in violation of a trust or allegiance… to be false or disloyal to… to lead astray; deceive." Your marriage covenant is a sacred pledge before God to be loyal to your wife alone; an alliance with sexual sin is "treason against" your bride, and is "leading her astray and deceiving her" into thinking she is the only woman your heart desires. The betrayal doesn't end until the deceit stops.

✦ By telling your wife, you force yourself to choose between her and sexual sin. Many men don't see their need to choose between lust and their wife until it's too late. Which one do you want to take care of you in your old age, porn or your wife?

✦ You rob your wife and yourself by not allowing her to support and pray for you in the battle. I am convinced that a man's most powerful ally in the battle against lust is his wife; she knows how to pray for you like no other person, and her grace and forgiveness will mean more to you than that of any man. She's your ally and best friend; it is lust that is your common enemy.

✦ Because you serve a holy God who commands us not to lie.

You should be accountable to your wife, but realize that women who are strong enough in the Lord to be an accountability partner for their husbands are rare. Tell her how you're doing when she asks, but don't feel that you need to tell her every time you're struggling with sexual fantasies or temptation—that's what your brothers are for. Men who attempt to make their wives an accountability partner put the full weight of the elephant on top of their marriage. Your wife can't and shouldn't attempt to fix you; her role is to support you. She has her own healing process to go through, and if you dump every struggle on her it will keep her stuck in pain. Conversely, you don't want to be the only person she confides to about her hurt. You're the source of her pain, so if you're the only support she has then her pain and anger remain in the marriage, building up for an explosion. You need her to have other women who she can process with, just as she needs you to have other men for accountability with lust. Having others around both of you is a safety valve that releases tension and pressure in the marriage so it can cool and heal.

Telling your wife you've committed adultery emotionally (with porn) or with another person won't be easy. But a marriage that's been tempered by the white-hot fires of sexual addiction grows deep, strong, and resilient, able to weather the toughest trials. While I will never say that my sexual sin is in any way a good thing, God used it to purify, realign, and strengthen our marriage. We tend to fight less over small disagreements, and resolve conflict on the big ones much quicker than before.

Once you allow your wife to see you as you are, faults and all, there's no more hiding, guilt or shame infesting the relationship. You'll both enjoy greater intimacy, and she will be your best friend. This is marriage as God intended it to be: open, vulnerable and loving; a wellspring of blessing for one man and his one woman.

I know you may be nervous about sharing your struggles with other men and your wife, but the blessings that come from living a transparent life are far greater than anything you will experience in isolation:

+ God promises that those who confess and forsake their sins will find compassion (Proverbs 28:13). Aren't mercy, understanding and forgiveness what you hope to receive if you expose your weaknesses? God *promises* you will receive it. You could tell the wrong person, like I did, but this won't stop Him from blessing you; He has no problem leading you to others who you can be open with and "find compassion." Ask Him to lead you to the right group or brother.

+ He promises that we will be healed if we confess our sins and others pray for us (James 5:16).

+ When we expose our dirty sins to others, the stain of shame is washed away from our heart. The compassion of those who "restore us with a spirit of gentleness" shows us we're not the unforgivable slime Satan had been telling us we were. The grace of others validates, encourages and lifts us up, setting us free to be who God has made us to be.

+ We no longer carry the heavy burden of our sin; we're freed from the need to hide, evade, and wear masks (Psalms 32:1–2).

+ Having others we are accountable to causes us to think twice before acting out sexually. I've heard the guys in Strength in Numbers say many times that having a group to come to has kept them from slipping the week prior, because they didn't want to have to tell us they'd fallen.

+ The chains of lust are broken. This doesn't mean the tyranny of sexual addiction is over; for true and lasting freedom all of the barriers that keep us from receiving God's grace in the heart must still be removed. But we're no longer the slave of lust we once were, and are working towards getting a new Master.

✦ We're not the lone stranger Christian we used to be. Like the TV show "Cheers," we have a place to go where "everyone knows our name" and we can find support and encouragement for any of the trials of life.

✦ We leave the insane wonderland of fantasy and find our way to the sweeping vistas of reality. When I was enslaved to lust I often coped with stress by running a fantasy (sexual or other) through my mind. Bringing our struggles to the light of others has a way of bringing us back to real life. The support and encouragement of others helped me regain my footing, and I discovered better ways to cope with life.

✦ Our wives and children are blessed when we're connected to others. When you participate in a group on a consistent basis you show your wife that you're serious about making her the only woman in your life. Your children will have a father who's less self-absorbed and pays more attention to them.

✦ You will smile and laugh again. You'll rediscover the interests and hobbies that were cast off when lust took over and find joy and contentment in the simple things in life again, like walking on the beach, hearing your kids scream "daddy" and hug you when you come home, or enjoying emotional and physical intimacy with your wife.

✦ You will learn to receive and give grace. The man who's exposed his sins and been accepted in spite of his faults is less critical of others; self-absorption fades away and he begins to be concerned for the needs of others.

✦ The church at-large is strengthened. Every man who walks free from lust is a living lighthouse of hope for others who struggle; more men who "walk in the light" (1 John 1:7) mean a stronger church, and a stronger church resists, shapes, and preserves our culture, rather than the other way around.

*Behold, how good and how pleasant it is for brothers
to dwell together in unity! It is like the precious oil upon
the head, coming down upon the beard, Even Aaron's beard,
coming down upon the edge of his robes. It is like the dew of
Hermon coming down upon the mountains of Zion; for there
the Lord commanded the blessing—life forever.*

PSALMS 133:1–3

You should get involved with a group or get an accountability partner before proceeding past chapter three; this book will be of little use to you if you try to go it alone. To find freedom from sexual sin, the support, encouragement, and prayers of others are mandatory, not optional; you will continue to fall in isolation. Remember God's words: "those who conceal their transgression will not prosper." Isolation is death, and "quarreling against sound wisdom."

Pride is often the last barrier between us and asking for the help of others; it was the case for me. I knew once I showed others who I really was that my reputation as a "good Christian" was shot. But what a relief it was to no longer have to fake it, or try to be something I could never be. Today I know that trading my pride, sin, and shame for all of the blessings mentioned above are a no-brainer, like giving someone a nickel for 10 one-ounce gold coins.

Those of us who know Christ are called to a bold life of uncompromising integrity, courage, and truth. Jesus modeled this when He walked our planet, and so have many others who have gone before us.

*Therefore, since we have so great a cloud of witnesses
surrounding us, let us also lay aside every encumbrance
and the sin which so easily entangles us, and let us run with*

endurance the race that is set before us, fixing our eyes on Jesus, the author and perfecter of faith, who for the joy set before Him endured the cross, despising the shame, and has sat down at the right hand of the throne of God. For consider Him who has endured such hostility by sinners against Himself, so that you will not grow weary and lose heart.

HEBREWS 12:1–3

chapter three

The Choice

~

"HAVE YOU MADE THE FOLLOWING DECISION ABOUT SIN—
THAT IT MUST BE COMPLETELY KILLED IN YOU? IT TAKES A LONG
TIME TO COME TO THIS POINT OF MAKING THIS COMPLETE
AND EFFECTIVE DECISION ABOUT SIN. IT IS HOWEVER THE GREATEST
MOMENT IN YOUR LIFE ONCE YOU DECIDE THAT SIN MUST DIE
IN YOU—NOT SIMPLY BE RESTRAINED, SUPPRESSED,
OR COUNTERACTED, BUT CRUCIFIED—JUST AS JESUS CHRIST DIED
FOR THE SIN OF THE WORLD. NO ONE CAN BRING ANYONE ELSE
TO THIS DECISION. WE MAY BE MENTALLY AND SPIRITUALLY
CONVINCED, BUT WHAT WE NEED TO DO IS ACTUALLY MAKE
THE DECISION THAT PAUL URGED TO DO IN ROMANS 6:6."[1]

Oswald Chambers

In 1957, Disney released the movie *Old Yeller*. Set in the 1860's, the story begins when a father leaves his wife and two sons, Travis, 14, and younger brother Arliss, to take care of their Texas ranch while he goes on a cattle run for three months. A big yellow dog wanders onto their ranch, and it's not long before he becomes a beloved member of their family.

Old Yeller (who is given his name because of the color of his coat) is both friend and protector; he helps Travis do his chores by chasing off scavengers, saves Arliss' life when he gets too close to a bear and her cub, and helps Travis when he falls from a tree into a herd of wild boar.

Late in the movie, a rabid wolf attacks Travis' mother, and Old Yeller comes to her rescue. Unfortunately, the dog is bitten and contracts rabies, a fatal viral disease which causes its host to become aggressive and attack without being provoked. Knowing the danger that a rabid dog poses to their family, Travis' mom wants to kill Old Yeller immediately. However, at Travis' urging, she agrees to keep the animal quarantined in a corn shed for a few weeks to see if it's okay.

As his beloved pet transforms into a violent enemy, Travis struggles with denial, not wanting to face the truth that his best friend now wants to tear him apart. He keeps Old Yeller's change of demeanor a secret, with the result that his younger brother is nearly killed when Arliss tries to release the rabid animal. Heartbroken, Travis finally accepts the reality of what he must do, and takes it upon himself to shoot Old Yeller.

Immediately after Old Yeller's death, Travis' father returns. Upon hearing what Travis went through, he encourages his son by reminding him that he did the right thing, telling him that life sometimes requires men to make tough, painful decisions.

Lust isn't a sweet golden retriever, nor is it your friend. It's a demonic werewolf disguised in soft, seductive lambskin, whose purpose is to destroy you, your marriage, and your family. To allow lust to live is to put your family at risk, just as Travis did when he allowed a rabid dog to endanger his family. Like Travis, you must come to grips with the fact that lust is out to destroy you and those you love; your only option is to kill it if you want to survive.

Many men are unaware of how dangerous the werewolf they're hiding can be. At a 2003 meeting of the American Academy of Matrimonial Lawyers, two-thirds of the 350 divorce lawyers in attendance said Internet porn contributed to more than half of the divorce cases they handled.[2] They also said that pornography "had an almost non-existent role in divorce just seven or eight years ago." Note that "just" pornography was the catalyst for divorce, not the physical act of adultery. Masturbating with porn is emotional adultery, and is just as devastating to a man's wife as an affair. The following is an email I received not long ago from one wife:

> *Back in August I was in contact with you when my husband Jim confessed his addiction with pornography to me. I told him I would support him in getting help but he refused, saying he has self-control and doesn't want or need help. I told him it was the only way our marriage could survive; we had separated numerous times because of his addiction in the past. I have filed for divorce. I am ready to be more vocal and speak out against this thing that is tearing families apart.*

Even though Jim's wife had separated from him multiple times, he was blind to how deeply he was hurting her. Jim said he didn't need help because he "had self-control," but this wasn't the real reason. His affection for the rabid animal that snarled at him from the darkness had become greater than his love for his family. In the end he lost everything.

The following post from one woman in the forums of the Blazing Grace website shows how her husband's love affair with lust affected her:

Sometimes when I'm hurting the worst and am crying, I ask God for a verse, something, anything to let me know that He's there; that He sees my pain and cares for my wounded heart, even though my husband doesn't. God has always given me immeasurably more than I could ask or imagine… usually on the floor of the bathroom, with a locked door, lots of Kleenex, my Bible and my journal. I remember spending lots of time in the Psalms then, as well… and sometimes reading a book I'd found at the Christian bookstore. Playing worship music is also helpful in lifting me out of despair and helping my heart to feel the love of God.

When we invite the werewolf of lust into our home, it attacks our wives. It shreds their self-esteem, leaving them feeling insecure and unloved by the one man who holds their heart. Like Jim's wife, they can endure the emotional attacks for only so long before they must leave in order to survive.

Remember Frank? He's the guy I told you about in the last chapter who first came to our group after his wife had kicked him out and was demanding a divorce. This was Frank's second marriage; his first wife, with whom he had two children, divorced him because of his sex addiction. What the kids go through often goes unnoticed; we have good friends who divorced this year from the husband's sex addiction, and it's been heart-breaking to watch their two sons flounder emotionally. The younger boy, who is 11 years old, repeatedly asks his mom when he's "going to get a new dad."

The werewolf doesn't stop attacking until he's mortally wounded every member of the family. Our kid's hearts are scarred for life when their father is torn from their home, setting them up for their own battle with sexual sin, drugs, or other problems:

+ "Three out of four teenage suicides occur in households where a parent has been absent."
Jean Beth Eshtain, "Family Matters: The Plight of America's Children." The Christian Century (July 1993).[3]

+ 75% of children/adolescents in chemical dependency hospitals are from single-parent families.
Center for Disease Control, Atlanta, GA.[4]

+ Boys living in a fatherless home are two to three times more likely to be involved in crime, drop out of school, and get divorced. Girls living in a fatherless home are two to three times more likely to become pregnant teenagers and have their marriages end in divorce.
"Heading Toward a Fatherless Society," by Barry Kliff, MSNBC News, www.msnbc.com, March 31, 1999.[5]

+ Almost 70% of young men in prison grew up without fathers in the home.
"American Agenda," World News Tonight with Peter Jennings, January 12, 1995.[6]

+ Women who are divorced are 300% more likely to file for bankruptcy.
"Women Rank First in Bankruptcy Filings," by Christine Dugas, USA Today, June 21, 1999.[7]

+ In 1998, the median income for single-mother households was $18,000. (The median income for married-couple families with children was $57,000.)
"Historical Income Tables-Families," Bureau of the Census, www.census.gov, Last revised October 4, 1999.[8]

Satan's goal is to get you hooked on porn or sexual sin so he can cut open your wife, tear your marriage apart, remove you from your family, and destroy your children. If you look back at the stories in chapter one you'll see that a number of

Christian marriages ended up in divorce. In our group we see men from every part of the church—including pastors—who have lost a family, are going through a divorce, or whose marriage is at a crisis point. Often, the cause is "just a little porn."

Dan is one of those men. He came to our group for the first time after his wife demanded a divorce because of his porn problem. Dan had spent his life in ministry; he'd taught many seminars at churches, led Bible studies, taught adult classes at church, and been involved in many other ways. After all his accomplishments, Dan was miffed and even bitter at why his wife was divorcing him "just because of porn." We saw the same thing that his wife probably did, and gently pointed it out to him; Dan was so focused on how good he was and what he wanted (porn) that he couldn't see how he was hurting his wife. Bitten by lust, Dan was blinded by the "All About Me" virus, just like Jim.

We never saw Dan again.

The demonic werewolf of lust will destroy your family if you try to keep it. You can't fool your wife into thinking you have enough self-control, like Jim tried to, or presume that your good works will somehow cause her to enjoy getting chewed up, like Dan did. Your wife knows that doing nothing means you want lust more than her. Like Old Yeller's owner, your choice is clear: let lust live and risk the devastating consequences, or *kill it.*

In Matthew 5:27–30, Jesus addresses the need for an all out assault on anything under our control that causes us to stumble in sexual sin:

> *You have heard that it was said 'You shall not commit adultery' but I say to you that everyone who looks at a woman with lust for her has already committed adultery with her in his heart. If your right eye makes you stumble tear it out and throw it from you; for it is better for you to lose one of the parts*

of your body, than for your whole body to be thrown into hell.
If your right hand makes you stumble cut it off and throw it
from you; for it is better for you to lose one of the parts of your
body, than for your whole body to be thrown into hell.

"Tear it out and throw it from you"… "cut it off and throw it from you"… "it's better to lose a part of your body than be thrown into hell." An eye that's been cut out of its socket can't be replaced; neither can a hand that's been severed. Tearing out an eye or cutting of a hand requires violent, brutal action; Jesus showed no concern for the resulting wound, or the severed members. The bloody body parts are to be "thrown away" like useless meat. We are to boldly approach the stumbling blocks of lust, viciously hack them off, and throw them away, regardless of any pain or loss.

Twice, Jesus said that cutting off the stumbling blocks is better than having "our whole body thrown into hell." I'm not going to take the time to address the salvation issue here, but it's obvious that Jesus is saying we can't have God and lust; we must choose which one we want. He left no comfort for those who intentionally make lust their god.

In Matthew 6:24 Jesus said:

"No one can serve two masters; for either he will hate
the one and love the other, or he will be devoted to one and
despise the other. You cannot serve God and wealth."

Although the context of this verse is about the love for money, the same principle applies to sexual sin, as Jesus clearly pointed out in Matthew 5:27–30. There's no fence we can sit on with God; either we cut off lust and make Him our first love, or we "hate God and love the other." The same choice must be made between our wives and lust.

Travis killed Old Yeller because he valued his family more than his dog, even though it had been a comfort to him. In the same way, our relationships with God and our wife must be far more precious than the short-term pleasure (and long-term misery) that lust provides.

So what does "killing lust" look like?

First, we need to understand who is responsible for pulling the trigger. Jesus commanded us to do the "tearing and cutting"; He never said He would do it for us.

When Rudy came to our group he was struggling with porn and masturbation on a weekly basis. Even though he consistently attended our meetings for the better part of a year, Rudy made little progress. He made few phone calls when tempted and didn't deal with the TV, which was a major source of temptation. In our meeting time Rudy would often complain that God wouldn't take his struggle with lust away from him, even though he didn't make much effort. At the last meeting he attended, Rudy admitted he wasn't willing to give up lust; he still had sexual fantasies that he wanted to act on and was intent on pursuing them.

Like Rudy, Sammy had a problem with porn addiction. During his second meeting, Sammy revealed he had a stash of porn magazines at home, and I asked him if he was willing to burn it. (It's better to burn pornography so that no one else finds it.) Sammy hemmed and hawed… "let me think about it… maybe…" Later in the meeting I asked him the same question a second, and then a third time, emphasizing that Sammy would never break free from lust if he didn't burn his porn stash. That was the last time we saw him.

God doesn't force us to give up our sin, and He doesn't take it away. If we're serious about finding freedom from lust, then we must walk the werewolf to the woodshed, place the barrel to its head, pull the trigger, and blow its brains out.

The process begins when we expose our sins to our brothers and stay out of isolation, as was discussed in the previous chapter. We "throw it away" when we give it to others.

We kick lust out of our marriage when we tell our wives about our struggle with sexual sin. To keep the rabid dog a secret from our wife is to hide it in the marriage—and put our family in danger. The same lady who I'd quoted earlier from our forums writes:

> *My husband allowed his fears over my reaction to cripple him, rather than trust God's truth that freedom comes when darkness is exposed by the light. Recently, the Lord allowed him to get caught, and because he didn't come to me on his own I'm having a hard time trusting him, and often wonder about the extent of his lies. He said he's acted out with porn and not another person, but he's lied so convincingly to me before that I have a hard time trusting he's been where he says he's been when he gets home late. It's difficult to heal when you don't know if you can believe your spouse about what's happened. Confession is always better for us wives than getting caught, because it builds trust by showing that our spouse doesn't want to lie to us anymore.*

Many men get stuck in the fear of their spouse's reaction, not realizing that their wives are willing to do anything to make the marriage work—as long as their husband is willing to kill lust. Jim's wife divorced him because he was unwilling to kill the rabid dog, not because he struggled with lust. If you let her, your wife will be your greatest ally.

Killing lust means we remove every stumbling block under our control, starting with the home:

> *I will give heed to the blameless way. When will You come to me? I will walk within my house in the integrity of my heart. I will set no worthless thing before my eyes; I hate the work of*

those who fall away; it shall not fasten its grip on me.
A perverse heart shall depart from me; I will know no evil.

PSALMS 101:2–4

Note the Psalmist's determination to live free from sin: "I will walk within my house... I will set no worthless thing... I hate the work... it shall not fasten it's grip on me... I will know no evil." He's not playing games or sitting on the fence when it comes to sexual purity, and is determined to do whatever it takes to keep anything out of his house that could "fasten its grip on him."

"Doing whatever it takes" means the porn stash gets burned; any CDs with pornography on them are broken and trashed. If you've downloaded porn from the Internet, wipe your hard drive clean by formatting it. You don't want any leftover files hanging around and popping up at the wrong time—like when one of your kids is on the computer.

If you can't get on the Internet without succumbing to temptation, work out a strategy with your wife as to how you will eliminate all possibility of you viewing porn on your computer. Some guys try to rely solely on their porn blocking software to keep them safe, but I have yet to hear of the man who couldn't get around it when he wanted to. In my opinion, porn blocking software works best as a safeguard for those who might unintentionally stumble onto it, i.e., children. This doesn't mean that porn blocking software isn't a good idea, it is, but it shouldn't be relied on as the final answer. The husband who struggles with Internet porn shouldn't be on the computer unless his wife is home, and awake. You can set up a password which only your wife would know in the security settings of the bios so the operating system won't load without the correct password.

Many have found software like Covenant Eyes (*www.covenanteyes.com*) to be effective. Covenant Eyes emails a list of every website you visit to the accountability partner(s) of your choice; they're also notified if the software is uninstalled or turned off. I recommend you have the notification emails sent to your wife and another guy; the knowledge that your wife will see every site you look at can be a powerful deterrent to lust, not unlike having her look over your shoulder as you're online.

If you do the above and still stumble, the computer needs to go. Focus on what you could lose, not what you're giving up. One friend of mine had his wife remove the computer from their apartment after he told her he'd slipped with Internet porn. After taking a few months for him to dry out, they brought the computer back and set passwords on their machine that only she knew. He's done fine since then. My friend told me he was glad his wife yanked their PC because he didn't have the strength to do it himself.

Note how I'm advocating that you work out a plan with your wife; she'll love it when you bring her into the battle with you. She can offer suggestions you might not have thought of, or like my friend, she can pull you up when you're too weak to fight. Having her on your side is much better than hiding and trying to fight in your own strength. "Two are better than one because they have a good return for their labor" (Ecclesiastes 4:9). It's a lot easier to aim and shoot when someone else holds the wolf's head; you also shorten the time it takes to rebuild trust when she sees you taking action.

If you find you're easily seduced by the flood of sexually charged images on TV, shut off the cable service and rip out the antenna; eliminate every incoming broadcast. It's far better to live free from temptation than have TV and risk the loss of your family. If you rent movies, be vigilant in avoiding any with sexual content.

If you've engaged in phone sex, have 900 number access from the home turned off. Ask you wife to keep you accountable by having her look at the phone bill every month.

Is your wife getting Victoria's Secret or other catalogs in the mail? Politely, yet firmly ask her to call the publishers and ask that they remove your address from their list. Ask your wife to be the one who checks the mail, every day. If magazine subscriptions such as *Sports Illustrated* or *People* are a problem, cancel them.

After you've removed every stumbling block from your home, take a hard look at any issues in the outside world. If hotel porn is a problem, don't turn on the TV when you travel, and call an accountability partner every night while you're away. I've heard of some guys who demand that the TV is removed from their room, but this may not always be practical. If none of this works and you still stumble, don't travel alone, or stop traveling, even if this means getting another job. Your holiness is more important to the Lord than your income, and He's not short on funds, jobs, or other resources.

Who has given to Me that I should repay him?
Whatever is under the whole heaven is Mine.

JOB 41:11

If you were having an affair, cut off all contact with the other person; burn any letters, delete every email, and trash anything they've given you. If they live nearby and the temptation is too much for you, move to another city.

Flee sexual immorality. Every other sin that a man
commits is outside the body, but the immoral man
sins against his own body.

1 CORINTHIANS 6:18

For some, certain parts of town are a trigger, perhaps where an adult bookstore or dancing bar is located. Keep away from these areas, or move.

My stumbling block was the TV, both at home and in hotels. I've been an NBA fanatic from my childhood years, and love watching the Los Angeles Lakers play. However, many games are broadcast late at night—when the phone sex and porn movie commercials start playing on the local channels. Although we had basic cable that didn't include movie channels like HBO or Showtime, the programming on regular TV alone was enough to trip me up. I also didn't need the temptation of knowing that I could order a pay-per-view porn movie at will. After discussing it with my wife, in 2002 we agreed to turn off all TV service in our home. Even though I can no longer watch my beloved Laker games, the freedom from temptation I enjoy in our home is a far greater blessing anything a sporting event has to offer. We still rent movies so it's not like we never watch TV, but all temptation has been eliminated.

When I travel alone the movie guide is placed in the drawer, and the TV stays off. I bring books to read, and a CD player with Christian music to fill the air with the sounds of God's peace. Flipping channels is what gets me started, so I treat the remote control as if it were a coiled rattlesnake. When we talk on the phone Michelle asks how I'm doing, and it always encourages me when she says she's praying for me. My accountability to my wife and the men in our group is a double-barreled shotgun of restraint, as I don't want to have to tell them I fell.

We need only cut off those things that cause us to stumble; if it's not a problem don't worry about it. I don't struggle with Internet porn; it's not a temptation for me like the TV and I don't have a porn blocker on my computer at work.

We're all wired differently, so we slip in different ways. If TV isn't an issue for you, then enjoy it. Legalism is when we give our list to others and demand they follow it; your list will be different from my list, and that's okay.

I know some of you are single, or divorced. I've addressed the past two chapters to the married because most men wait until marriage before they deal with their sexual sin. The truths we've covered are no different for the single than the married; you who are single are ahead of the game in that you can save your future wife from having to go through the hell that so many women endure. If there is a stumbling block you need to deal with, please don't wait; cut it off now.

Let's be honest; part of what makes it so hard to kill lust is that we like it. We make lust our comfort, love, and best friend, and wonder "what will take lust's place once I kill it?" Like Travis, we don't want to kill the rabid dog, even though it poses a lethal threat to us and those we love.

This book is about finding the life and love which you've tried to find in lust. Such life comes only from God, and He won't compete with sin. The choice is now set before you in clear, black and white terms. Like Travis, you have a decision to make; kill the rabid dog, or risk the consequences.

Shotgun, anyone?

If it is disagreeable in your sight to serve the Lord,
choose for yourselves today whom you will serve:
whether the gods which your fathers served which were
beyond the River, or the gods of the Amorites in whose land you
are living; but as for me and my house, we will serve the Lord."

JOSHUA 24:15

chapter four

The Fatal Tragedy

~

"THE MORAL LAW, ORDAINED BY GOD, DOES NOT MAKE ITSELF WEAK
TO THE WEAK BY EXCUSING OUR SHORTCOMINGS. IT REMAINS
ABSOLUTE FOR ALL TIME AND ETERNITY. IF WE ARE NOT AWARE OF
THIS, IT IS BECAUSE WE ARE LESS THAN ALIVE. ONCE WE DO REALIZE
THIS, OUR LIFE IMMEDIATELY BECOMES A FATAL TRAGEDY."[1]

Oswald Chambers

I t was late fall, 1998. I'd gone on a business trip and binged
on porn movies in the hotel rooms, again, albeit without
masturbating. Even though I hadn't had self-sex, the images,
filth and shame flowing through me were no less intense.

Not long after returning home, I met with Jim, a guy from
the secular 12-step group I'd been attending, for lunch. (In
the '90s, Christ-centered support groups for sexual addiction
were extremely rare.) After I told him what I'd done, Jim said
"at least you didn't act out," meaning that, according to the
sobriety definition of the group I was still "sober." For the
first time in eight years of "working the steps," it hit me that
the 12-step program had taken me as far as it could.

One problem was their definition of sexual sobriety. It started with "no sex with self or other persons other than the married spouse," which was okay, and then they had a weird statement about "true sobriety meaning progressive victory over lust." Since "progressive victory" was hard to grab onto, (or really, meaningless) everyone focused on the physical aspect of the definition. Thus, a man was "sober" if he hadn't masturbated or had sex with another person outside of marriage. Guys with one year or more of sobriety were revered as if they were a prophet, and newcomers flocked to them for their secrets.

In the early 90's when I first got involved in the 12-step program, I jumped in with both feet and accumulated 18 months of sobriety. Now *I* was one of the chosen ones who the others fawned over. I started leading meetings and sponsoring others, dispensing my wisdom like Plato. I had become the "Oracle of Sobriety," or so I thought.

The American Heritage Dictionary of the English Language defines sobriety as "Moderation in or abstinence from consumption of alcoholic liquor or use of drugs." Even though I'd abstained from porn, masturbation, and sex outside of marriage for a year and a half, there was still a nagging emptiness inside that gnawed at me. That spiritual vacuum won out on a business trip to Canada, when I lost my 18 months of sobriety on a phone sex and masturbation binge. Overnight, my status as "O wise one" vanished, and it was back to Square One with Those-Not-Worthy-of-the- 30-Day-Chip.

I bounced back quickly, and gained another three years of sobriety. With three years to my name, it seemed to me the others should have bowed down every time I walked into a meeting. How could I fall again, I thought, after going so long without acting out?

We moved from Los Angeles to Colorado Springs in 1995. With my support base gone, the ever-present vacuum of emptiness intensified into a loud roar. I fell hard, and lost my sobriety again on a bender of porn and masturbation. This time, I couldn't get back up, and slid into a three-year period of binging, shame and misery.

It was the end of that third year when I met Jim for lunch. When he told me I was "sober" even though I'd looked at porn, the light went on that I was after something deeper and more powerful than mere physical abstinence; I wanted the power within to say no to every temptation or lustful thought. Eight years of focusing on the externals had provided me with temporary relief, but not freedom; I was still a slave to sexual sin in my heart.

Purity and sobriety aren't the same thing. The American Heritage Dictionary defines purity as:

1. The quality or condition of being pure.

2. Freedom from sin or guilt; innocence; chastity.

A man can abstain from sin, but still have a dark, lonely, lust-filled heart. Weeds aren't eliminated until someone digs deep, exposes the roots, and gets rid of the entire plant. If a man cuts off the top of the weed but leaves the roots intact, the top will eventually grow back. When Jesus set God's standard for sexual purity He had something much deeper than the top of the weed in mind:

> *You have heard that it was said, 'You shall not commit*
> *adultery'; but I say to you that everyone who looks*
> *at a woman with lust for her has already committed*
> *adultery with her in his heart.*

MATTHEW 5:27–28

In the verses above, note that Jesus transitioned from the physical to the spiritual when He set *The Standard* for sexual purity. While men may focus on the externals to define "sobriety," God looks at the heart, for this is where "evil thoughts, murders, adulteries, fornications, thefts, false witness and slanders" come from (Mathew 15:19). Jesus left no loopholes; in the instant we lust after another person we've sinned, or "lost our sobriety." There's no "three second rule," where we can gaze at another woman with lustful intent for three seconds until it becomes sin as some have promoted.

With God's standard of sexual purity, I'm forced to my knees in surrender. The white flag is raised, and the battle is over before it starts. I can go to support groups and remove the TV from my home, but I can't clean up my heart. It'd be like trying to plug a dam with 1,000 holes on my own, or trying open heart surgery on myself. There are too many leaks, and I'm no doctor.

I get emails from guys complaining that I advocate abstinence from masturbation, and can hear it now: "that's impossible; who can measure up to a standard like *that*??! No one can clean up their heart!" I agree. If we're honest, God's standard for sexual purity *is* impossible, and I believe He intended it that way. Since only God can transform a filthy, lustful, and self-absorbed heart into a pure one, I'm forced to abandon all hope in my abilities and lean hard on Him.

Who can say, "I have cleansed my heart,
I am pure from my sin"?
PROVERBS 20:9

In the churches I grew up in, much of the emphasis was on knowing Bible doctrine and trying to live up to it to please God; I spent a lot of my early Christian life trying to "be good enough" to earn His approval. My involvement in the 12-step groups, in part, was an attempt to stop sinning so He would love me. When I got involved with ministry, it was to "be the good Christian," and look good in front of others; I knew a lot of Bible, so it was easy to fake it and say all the right words at church.

I had become successful in the business world through hard work and gut-level intuition, and brought this mentality in my efforts to conquer sin. Focusing all of my drive and willpower in trying to be sober worked, for a little while... while I gauged my progress from man's standard of abstinence.

I've talked with pastors and ministry leaders who struggle with porn and think they're okay because of external circumstances, like I did. They judge themselves by their knowledge of theology, how big their church is, and the praise of their flock. Many are gifted communicators who know how to turn a crowd. Like me, they look good on the outside, but, their little secret reveals there's something wrong inside.

Peter had it made. Jesus had told him "I will give you the keys of the kingdom of heaven; and whatever you bind on earth shall have been bound in heaven, and whatever you loose on earth shall have been loosed in heaven" (Matthew 16:19). Peter had gone on short-term missions trips, casting out demons and healing the sick (Matthew 10). He'd been promised a throne with Jesus in Heaven (Matthew 19:28). Peter had power, authority, success in ministry, and wonderful promises for the future.

Then, the night before He was crucified, Jesus told Peter he would deny Him three times. Peter balked, promising "even if I have to die with You, I will not deny You" (Matthew 26:35). How could a man from whom demons fled fall so easily?

But Peter denied the Lord three times, the last with cursing. Broken by his public failure, Peter "went out and wept bitterly" (Matthew 26:75). All of his success and abilities were now meaningless; there was no denying that Peter was ruined.

For I know that nothing good dwells in me,
that is, in my flesh; for the willing is present in me,
but the doing of the good is not.

ROMANS 7:18

Not long after I met with Jim, I got alone with God. I'd spent eight years in the 12-step program, more than 10 years in counseling (with Christian counselors), had read plenty of books, been to healing conferences, been hypnotized, prayed and read my Bible daily, led groups, mentored others, been involved in successful ministry and all of my efforts had rewarded me with—nothing. Freefalling in despair, I cried out, "Lord I've done all this stuff and nothing's worked. Either You're the God You say You are who can change lives, or this whole Christianity thing is a crock; you're my last hope. I don't even know if I really know you."

In that moment, God held a mirror up to my heart. It was a deep, dark hole, walled off with pride, corrupted with lust, and filled with selfishness. There wasn't anything good there, not even a glimmer of light. I wasn't "the good Christian" I'd thought I was and had spent much of my life trying to be; it was all a lie, a show to fool myself and others into thinking I was "it." I sat on the floor, crying, not knowing what to do next.

The eye is the lamp of the body; so then if your eye is clear, your
whole body will be full of light. But if your eye is bad, your
whole body will be full of darkness. If then the light that is in
you is darkness, how great is the darkness!

MATTHEW 6:22–23

The prophet Isaiah knew the despair that comes from seeing a black heart:

*In the year of King Uzziah's death I saw the Lord sitting
on a throne, lofty and exalted, with the train of His robe
filling the temple. Seraphim stood above Him, each having
six wings: with two he covered his face, and with two he covered
his feet, and with two he flew. And one called out to another
and said, "Holy, Holy, Holy, is the Lord of hosts, the whole
earth is full of His glory." And the foundations of the
thresholds trembled at the voice of him who called out, while
the temple was filling with smoke. Then I said, "Woe is me,
for I am ruined! Because I am a man of unclean lips,
and I live among a people of unclean lips;
for my eyes have seen the King, the Lord of hosts."*

Isaiah 6:1–5

God's holy presence contrasted Isaiah's sinful state so
sharply that he realized his heart was as soiled and corrupt as
his mouth. If asked, Isaiah would probably have admitted that
he liked swearing; his heart was so evil that he enjoyed sin.
When I saw my black heart, I had to admit the same; I had
struggled with giving sexual sin up because I loved it, even
though I hated the shame and conviction that came afterwards.

In Luke 18:9–14, Jesus gave a picture of two men; one who
relied on his abilities and good works, and another who faced
the true condition of his heart:

*And He also told this parable to some people who trusted in
themselves that they were righteous, and viewed others with
contempt: "Two men went up into the temple to pray, one a
Pharisee and the other a tax collector. The Pharisee stood and
was praying this to himself: 'God, I thank You that I am not
like other people: swindlers, unjust, adulterers, or even like this
tax collector. I fast twice a week; I pay tithes of all that I get.'
But the tax collector, standing some distance away, was even
unwilling to lift up his eyes to heaven, but was beating his*

breast, saying, 'God, be merciful to me, the sinner!'
I tell you, this man went to his house justified rather
than the other; for everyone who exalts himself will
be humbled, but he who humbles himself will be exalted."

Luke states that the parable Jesus told was to those who "trusted in themselves." If I was the Pharisee Jesus mentioned in this verse, my "prayer to myself" would have sounded something like this: "God, I thank You that I am not like other people; I'm not a prude goody-goody who can't talk about the real issues of life like other Christians. I attend two support groups a week and I'm sexually sober (I have the sobriety chips to prove it); I've served in ministry, know the Bible, make good money, and am an honest man. I can do a lot of good things for you. I'm not proud like other Christians who come off like they know it all."

When God showed me my heart, I was forced to look at my cold, critical, judging spirit. I was constantly putting others down in my heart, even when I had my Sunday face on. I judged other Christians who hadn't had struggles with drugs or sex as shallow. I was continuously picking my wife apart. My employers or co-workers weren't as smart as I was. Churches that didn't deal with sexual sin were weak, afraid to deal with the truth. Churches that did talk about sexual sin were Bible thumpers. It was always easy to find a way to tear someone else apart so I could say, "God, I thank You that I am not like other people."

After the Lord placed the mirror in front of my heart, what others were like no longer mattered; it hurt too much. Like the second man in Jesus' parable, all I had left was to cry out "God, be merciful to me, the sinner!"

For the struggler with sexual sin to be able to stand before Almighty God and claim "sobriety" before Him, he must measure up to Jesus' perfect standard of sexual purity. There can be no lust in the heart for even a second. If we're honest, we have to admit we can't do it, no matter how many support groups we attend, how much time we spend in the Word, or ministry we're involved in.

After working with other men, I know there are few who have the courage to face their brokenness. They may talk about being a sinner in cognitive terms, but they haven't faced the fact that they've spent their life building a monument to self on a foundation of sand. They may know Romans 3:9–18, but it's theology stored in their mind, not the reality of their life.

> *What then? Are we better than they? Not at all;*
> *for we have already charged that both Jews and Greeks*
> *are all under sin; as it is written, "There is none righteous,*
> *not even one; there is none who understands, there is none who*
> *seeks for God; all have turned aside, together they have become*
> *useless; there is none who does good, there is not even one.*
> *Their throat is an open grave, with their tongues they keep*
> *deceiving, the poison of asps is under their lips;*
> *whose mouth is full of cursing and bitterness;*
> *their feet are swift to shed blood, destruction*
> *and misery are in their paths, and the path of peace*
> *they have not known. There is no fear of God before their eyes."*

Those who haven't faced their brokenness may not be "swift to shed blood," but they're quick to turn to porn, like I was. "Misery is in their path," and they've not been down the "path of peace." Deep down, they don't want to give up the idea that they can be good enough to earn God's love, especially after all the good ministry work they've done. Facing the truth would be too painful.

Pride doesn't die easily; mine didn't. Remember Dan from the last chapter? He'd built his whole life on the ministry he'd been involved in, yet when his wife confronted him on his porn problem he got angry. If you read through the Gospels, you'll see that the Pharisees got angry when Jesus confronted them with their self-reliance and self-righteousness. Pride blows up when it's exposed and confronted. Dan's good works couldn't hide the fact that his life was a fatal tragedy.

Some use false humility to throw others off the scent; "I'm a piece of trash; I've messed up too much for God to love me." They go around in perpetual mourning, looking over their shoulders to see who might be interested in joining their pity party. Those who've faced the darkness and declared bankruptcy don't care about pity; it won't pay off their creditors.

In Revelations 3:14–22, Jesus confronted an entire church for their self-reliance:

To the angel of the church in Laodicea write: The Amen, the faithful and true Witness, the Beginning of the creation of God, says this: "I know your deeds, that you are neither cold nor hot; I wish that you were cold or hot. So because you are lukewarm, and neither hot nor cold, I will spit you out of My mouth. Because you say, 'I am rich, and have become wealthy, and have need of nothing,' and you do not know that you are wretched and miserable and poor and blind and naked, I advise you to buy from Me gold refined by fire so that you may become rich, and white garments so that you may clothe yourself, and that the shame of your nakedness will not be revealed; and eye salve to anoint your eyes so that you may see. Those whom I love, I reprove and discipline; therefore be zealous and repent. Behold, I stand at the door and knock; if anyone hears My voice and opens the door, I will come in to him and will dine with him, and he with Me. He who overcomes, I will grant to him to sit down with Me on My throne, as I also overcame and sat down with My Father on His throne. He who has an ear, let him hear what the Spirit says to the churches.

Laodicea was an economic center known for its wool industry, production of eye salve, and banking. The city's material prosperity had lulled the church into a state of self-sufficiency and lukewarm complacency. (Note that Jesus told them to buy eye salve from Him so they could see—an obvious reference to their focus on trade.) In telling them to buy "gold refined by fire" (i.e., a pure heart) from Him, Jesus confronted the Laodicean church with the utter depravity of their self-sufficiency.

My success in the business world and ministry had a "Laodicean effect" on me. Even though I knew God's Word condemned material success as a gage of righteousness, I allowed the material pleasures of life to seduce me into the idea that I "had need of nothing." Add the corruption of porn addiction to the mix, and the stage for lukewarm Christianity was set.

Those who trust in their abilities and effort, like the Pharisees, or believe they're okay because of ministry, like Dan, or are seduced to apathy by material prosperity, like the church of Laodicea, don't see their desperate need for God. It is the "wretched and poor" who cry out "I am ruined... God be merciful to me the sinner"—and receive grace and blessing in abundance. Look at what happened after Isaiah admitted his brokenness:

Then one of the seraphim flew to me with a burning coal in his hand, which he had taken from the altar with tongs. He touched my mouth with it and said, "Behold, this has touched your lips; and your iniquity is taken away and your sin is forgiven." Then I heard the voice of the Lord, saying, "Whom shall I send, and who will go for Us?" Then I said, "Here am I. Send me!" He said, "Go, and tell this people..."

ISAIAH 6:6–9

The American Heritage Dictionary describes iniquity as "gross immorality or injustice; wickedness." In a moment, the Lord burned away and forgave all Isaiah's sin. Once freed, God used Isaiah powerfully to speak to the nation of Israel.

Note the progression that took place; Isaiah approached the Lord and was convicted by God's holiness; in despair, Isaiah realized his condition was hopeless, and he confessed his utter bankruptcy. The Lord cleansed Isaiah's heart, and asked "who shall I send?"; Isaiah eagerly responded to God's call. Isaiah's confession of brokenness was the doorway through which God changed his life and used Him.

Peter walked through the same doorway of brokenness that Isaiah did. After Jesus restored him, Peter was used of God to lead some 3,000 men and women to Christ in Acts 2; it was Peter through whom God first presented the gospel to the Gentiles, and Peter through whom God penned two books of the Bible (First and Second Peter).

Enter through the narrow gate; for the gate is wide and the way is broad that leads to destruction, and there are many who enter through it. For the gate is small and the way is narrow that leads to life, and there are few who find it.

MATTHEW 7:13–14

I believe there are so few who find the small and narrow way to life because many are not willing to face the painful truth of their brokenness. As the road narrows, all self sufficiency, lust, and the idea that we can measure up to God's standards must be left behind.

Paul wrote of the blessings of that come from accepting his weakness:

Because of the surpassing greatness of the revelations, for this reason, to keep me from exalting myself, there was given me a thorn in the flesh, a messenger of Satan to torment me—to

*keep me from exalting myself! Concerning this I implored the
Lord three times that it might leave me. And He has said
to me, "My grace is sufficient for you, for power is perfected in
weakness." Most gladly, therefore, I will rather boast about
my weaknesses, so that the power of Christ may dwell in me.
Therefore I am well content with weaknesses, with insults,
with distresses, with persecutions, with difficulties,
for Christ's sake; for when I am weak, then I am strong.*

2 CORINTHIANS 12:7–10

Paul was allowed to suffer with a "thorn in the flesh" to
keep him from buying into the lie that anything God had
accomplished through Paul or blessed him with was because
of Paul's abilities. For Paul to be seduced into self-sufficiency
would have been a disaster, as we know from Peter's story.
Although the context of Paul accepting his weakness wasn't
a struggle with sin, the principal is the same as what we saw
with Isaiah and Peter: to have the power of Christ in our
heart we must depend only on God; all confidence in our
abilities must be set aside.

Facing our brokenness isn't something to be feared, but
embraced. When we renounce all self-sufficiency and vacate
the throne room of our heart, the door is opened for the Lord
to clean up our heart and take residence there.

It is God alone who cleans up a sinful heart, not going to
support groups or counseling:

*Moreover, I will give you a new heart and put a new spirit
within you; and I will remove the heart of stone from your flesh
and give you a heart of flesh.*

EZEKIEL 36:26

Facing our brokenness is the beginning of life, and freedom from sexual sin; the end of lust's reign in our heart and
the beginning of God's. Six months after God held a mirror

up to my heart and I made Him my only hope, He set me free from the slavery to sexual sin.

The sacrifices of God are a broken spirit;
a broken and a contrite heart, O God, You will not despise.

PSALMS 51:17

...for we are the true circumcision, who worship
in the Spirit of God and glory in Christ Jesus
and put no confidence in the flesh...

PHILIPPIANS 3:3

Once freed from the burden of a reputation to carry and maintain, confessing sins and asking for the help and prayer of others is much easier for those who "put no confidence in their flesh." Since they understand that everyone is broken, they're slower to judge others, and they cease trying to manipulate and control. Life gets easier, and freer, and they can move faster. With the Lord guiding them, new vistas open up, and life becomes an exhilarating (and sometimes challenging) adventure of faith. In short, they've discovered the blessing that comes from accepting their brokenness. Perhaps this is why Jesus said:

Blessed are the poor in spirit,
for theirs is the kingdom of heaven.

MATTHEW 5:3

Going to accountability groups and doing the things we've talked about in the past two chapters are the beginning of the road to grace and freedom from sexual sin, not the end. My hope is that you will set out on the adventure of faith and place all of your hope on God. If you've never faced your brokenness and are ready to, enter the throne room of the Living God and ask Him to reveal the true condition of your heart to you. Write what He shows you in your journal, and meditate on all of the verses in this chapter. Consider His strict standard for sexual purity, and whether you can attain it by anything you can do. Think on how God responds to the broken, and the blessings He's promised to those who quit playing the Christian game. And then, my prayer is that you will leave your burden by the side of the road and move on.

Search me, O God, and know my heart;
try me and know my anxious thoughts;
and see if there be any hurtful way in me,
and lead me in the everlasting way.

PSALMS 139:23–24

He who trusts in his own heart is a fool,
but he who walks wisely will be delivered.

PROVERBS 28:26

I have been crucified with Christ; and it is no longer
I who live, but Christ lives in me; and the life which
I now live in the flesh I live by faith in the Son of God,
who loved me and gave Himself up for me.

GALATIANS 2:20

c h a p t e r   f i v e

Turn and Connect

~

MEN, WHY ARE YOU DOING THESE THINGS? WE ARE ALSO MEN
OF THE SAME NATURE AS YOU, AND PREACH THE GOSPEL TO YOU
THAT YOU SHOULD TURN FROM THESE VAIN THINGS TO A LIVING
GOD, WHO MADE THE HEAVEN AND THE EARTH AND THE SEA
AND ALL THAT IS IN THEM.

Acts 14:15

In his prime, Iron Mike Tyson was a ferocious fighting machine with phenomenal punching power. In 1985, at the age of 20, he won the WBC title from Trevor Berbick in less than six minutes. Michael Spinks, an undefeated former champion, was knocked out by Tyson in 91 seconds. Carl "The Truth" Williams went down in 93 seconds. By 1990, Tyson had a 37–0 record with 33 knockouts.

I remember watching Tyson in one of his early fights, thinking about just how hard he could hit. There was a loud smack when Tyson connected with his opponent's face, and his head snapped back like it'd been hit with a cannonball. The thought of taking a shot like that gave me the jitters.

Imagine getting into the ring with Mike Tyson when he was at the top of his game. The bell rings. Tyson calmly walks up to you in his trademark black trunks, grinning and showing his gold tooth, his hands down at his sides in mockery of you. You know that if this guy hits you it's all over, so you charge him and swing hard. Tyson deftly swivels his torso and avoids your punch, still grinning, hands at his sides. You panic and swing wildly, but Tyson dances around your every blow with ease. Over the next few minutes you throw a frenzy of punches, but nothing connects.

Now you're exhausted; your arms feel like they're made of lead and your guard is down. Still grinning, Tyson launches a right cross to your jaw that connects with incredible force; the room starts spinning, and turns black as you drop to the floor.

Fighting sexual thoughts and temptation is like taking on Mike Tyson. Lust is far stronger, faster, smarter and more experienced than you are. The power behind it has been around for centuries, and it's knocked out millions. Satan's strategy is to get you in the ring with lust, because once you start swinging he knows he'll win; *he wants you fighting it.* The final outcome may take a few rounds, but it doesn't matter; he knows that once you wear yourself out, it's lights out.

I've tried several different methods of dealing with sexual temptation over the years.

1. Ignoring the thoughts. This doesn't work because they keep coming back, often with greater intensity.

2. Quoting Scripture. I once heard someone say that since Jesus quoted God's word when He was tempted by Satan in the desert, we should use the same strategy in resisting temptation. I tried this and it sometimes worked, for a little while, but the thoughts always came storming back.

3. "Commanding the devil to leave." There have been a few instances where this worked, which may have meant the attack was purely spiritual. However, most of the time I'm battling my own flesh and brokenness in addition to any outside spiritual influence, making this approach ineffective.

4. Calling a friend (see chapter two). This helps if I'm able to get someone on the phone immediately, but what happens if no one's available? I can't just let lustful thoughts run roughshod over me until I can talk to someone; it might be too late by then. Besides, Jesus commanded us not to commit adultery in our heart, so I need a way to cope with the thoughts as temptation hits, not after I've sinned.

There are no verses in Scripture in which we are commanded to conquer or even attempt to conquer sexual temptation by our *own* strength or willpower. When Joseph was tempted by Potiphar's wife in Genesis 39, he ran. If he would have stayed to resist her she would have touched him provocatively, sparking the flames of sexual desire. Paul confirmed the flight versus fight approach in 1 Corinthians 6:18 when he wrote we are to "flee (sexual) immorality."

Note how the Lord calls us to deal with sin in the following verses:

> *Yet the Lord warned Israel and Judah through*
> *all His prophets and every seer, saying, "Turn from your evil*
> *ways and keep My commandments, My statutes according*
> *to all the law which I commanded your fathers, and which*
> *I sent to you through My servants the prophets."*
>
> 2 KINGS 17:13

> *...and (if) My people who are called by My name humble*
> *themselves and pray and seek My face and turn from their*

wicked ways, then I will hear from heaven,
will forgive their sin and will heal their land.

2 CHRONICLES 7:14

Turn away my eyes from looking at vanity,
and revive me in Your ways.

PSALMS 119:37

Do not be wise in your own eyes;
fear the Lord and turn away from evil.

PROVERBS 3:7

Turn to Me and be saved, all the ends of the earth;
For I am God, and there is no other.

ISAIAH 45:22

And I said, "Who are You, Lord?" and the Lord said,
"I am Jesus whom you are persecuting. But get up and stand on
your feet; for this purpose I have appeared to you, to appoint
you a minister and a witness not only to the things which you
have seen, but also to the things in which I will appear to you;
rescuing you from the Jewish people and from the Gentiles,
to whom I am sending you, to open their eyes so that they may
turn from darkness to light and from the dominion of Satan
to God, that they may receive forgiveness of sins and an inheri-
tance among those who have been sanctified by faith in Me."

ACTS 26:15–18

God calls us to *turn away* from sin and *to Him*, after which
He will forgive our sin, "heal our land," and "revive us in His
ways." In the battle against the Mike Tysons of sexual temptation and thoughts, we don't face lust, try to negotiate with
it, or fight it. As soon as we're tempted, we immediately turn
away from the thought and then connect with God, setting

our mind on Him and asking for His help and power. I call this the *turn and connect* approach.

Here's what "turn and connect" looks like: I'm sitting at my office and a picture of an old girlfriend pops up in my mind. Immediately, I turn to God; I imagine Him, seated on the great white throne in Heaven in all of His majestic glory and splendor. From within I call out "Lord, create in me a clean heart; I don't want any other women except for the wife you've given me." My focus is now on God (and I've even brought my wife into the picture); I've turned away from the lustful thought and connected with the Lord and His power. Not an ounce of energy was wasted on fighting; the temptation fades away as I come into the Lord's presence, and the battle is over.

Rehearsing scripture alone doesn't work because there's no connection with the Power behind the words. Isaiah 45:22 says *Turn to Me and be saved*, not "quote the Bible." We are turning to the Living God, Who hears us, cares for us, and can overcome every temptation; it is He who gives us the power to "walk in the light."

but if we walk in the Light as He Himself is in the Light, we have fellowship with one another, and the blood of Jesus His Son cleanses us from all sin.

1 JOHN 1:7

I am the vine, you are the branches; he who abides in Me and I in him, he bears much fruit, for apart from Me you can do nothing.

JOHN 15:5

Pray without ceasing

1 THESSALONIANS 5:17

Abiding in Jesus (turn and connect) is to be our way of life, not a one-time event. When "we pray without ceasing," He provides the power to "walk in the light," free from sin. "Apart from me, you can do nothing," said Jesus; the Christian life is minute-by-minute dependence on the Living God and His power. We are not strong enough to fight the Mike Tysons of temptation, so when the battle starts we must lean heavily on the Lord. It is here, in the heat of battle, where our faith is fire-tested and made true (1 Peter 1:6–7).

Create in me a clean heart, O God, and renew
a steadfast spirit within me... Restore to me the joy
of Your salvation and sustain me with a willing spirit.

PSALMS 51:10,12

I often ask the Lord for the blessings of these verses in the midst of temptation, as they give voice to my desires. When I ask Him to "create in me a clean heart," I'm acknowledging my inability to do so and my complete dependence on Him for freedom from sin. When I'm shaken or attacked with fear or doubt, I need Him to stabilize me with a steadfast spirit. And, I want to live in the joy of His light and love so I ask that He "restores me with the joy of His salvation."

The process of asking the Lord to "create in me a clean heart" many times over the years has retrained my mind. In the past I would turn to lustful thoughts by reflex when hit with temptation; today, "create in me a clean heart..." pops up at even the threat of temptation.

Turn and connect is just as powerful in the physical world. When an attractive woman crosses my path I'll immediately turn to God in my heart, saying something like "Lord I want you; You're my source of life, not her. Create in me a clean heart." Ultimately, lust is an attempt to fill the emptiness inside with another person; by acknowledging the Lord as my source of life, I'm looking to Him for comfort, life and love, not another broken person.

When encountering women who are not my wife, I look them in the eyes, not their body parts; I may notice their figure in my field of vision, but I don't let my eyes "drop, lock and roll." There is one woman in this world whose body I allow my eyes to gaze over, and that's Michelle's. To gaze on another woman's body is to paw her with the eyes.

> *I have made a covenant with my eyes;*
> *how then could I gaze at a virgin?*
>
> JOB 31:1

In December of 2003, I took three of my kids to a beauty salon to buy a gift certificate as a Christmas present for Michelle. It was a work night, and I was worn out from the day; a beauty salon was the last place I wanted to go, especially with three restless kids in tow. I entered the salon; where two girls in their 20's stood at the counter, dressed to kill. The one who helped me wore thin, skin tight clothes meant to accentuate every curve. The pull to look was intense; I kept my eyes locked on her face and cried out from within: "Father, You know there's something in me that wants to look at her figure, please help me; create in me a clean heart." The pull didn't let up, but neither did I; I continued turning to the Lord throughout the time I was in the salon. By God's grace and power I didn't maul that girl with my eyes, even though my flesh was screaming for it; if I'd have resisted on my own the chances are high I would have given in.

> *For though we walk in the flesh, we do not war according*
> *to the flesh, for the weapons of our warfare are not of the flesh,*
> *but divinely powerful for the destruction of fortresses.*
> *We are destroying speculations and every lofty thing raised up*

against the knowledge of God, and we are taking every thought captive to the obedience of Christ

2 CORINTHIANS 10:3–5

It's critical that we "take every thought captive" and turn to God the instant temptation hits; once you give lust an inch of daylight it charges the opening and goes for a touchdown. If I would have waited a few seconds before drawing on God's strength that night in the salon, I probably would have lusted with my eyes, which could have taken me to sexual fantasy, the sin of adultery in the heart, and maybe worse. To delay turning to God is playing with lust, and messing with this fire gets us burned; we must turn to God the instant temptation hits.

Playing with a mental image of a woman with clothes on, by the way, can still be adultery. When we use an image to draw life or comfort from, it's the same as worshipping it, and worshipping an image of a woman is idolatry and adultery, regardless of clothing. The intent is as important as the object.

When we train ourselves to feed on Jesus for life, love and comfort, our desires change, and we find ourselves hungering for God instead of lust. Temptation, which is meant to cause us to sin, now has the unintended effect of drawing us closer to the Lord.

Another benefit of turn and connect is that it cleanses our imagination. A man who has spent years soaking his mind in porn has trained his imagination to conjure up the images of lust. When we picture Heaven as we're connecting with God, we're retraining our imagination to form images that provoke worship and awe of the Living God.

Read through the following from Revelations 1:12–17:

Then I turned to see the voice that was speaking with me. And having turned I saw seven golden lampstands;

and in the middle of the lampstands I saw one like
a son of man, clothed in a robe reaching to the feet,
and girded across His chest with a golden sash.
His head and His hair were white like white wool, like snow;
and His eyes were like a flame of fire. His feet were
like burnished bronze, when it has been made to glow
in a furnace, and His voice was like the sound of many waters.
In His right hand He held seven stars, and out of His
mouth came a sharp two-edged sword;
and His face was like the sun shining in its strength.
When I saw Him, I fell at His feet like a dead man.

The Jesus we see in these verses is nothing like the long haired hippie many have portrayed him to be. Picture a Person whose face beams with light so powerful that it's like looking at the mid-day sun. He has eyes with such intensity that they smolder like fire; His hair is white, not like an old man's hair, but fresh snow. His feet are bronze in color; smooth and polished in appearance. He is clothed in a spotless, floor-length white robe with a gleaming gold sash around the chest. His voice has many layers; like none we've heard before. John had been so comfortable with Jesus that He'd leaned on his chest at the last supper, yet at the blazing appearance of the Son of God he dropped to the floor "like a dead man."

When I picture the Lord in His awesome glory, my imagination is transformed from corruption to something holy, powerful and wonderful. My faith is set ablaze, because a God like this has no problem vaporizing the Mike Tysons of sexual temptation. Lust, which was so big, intimidating and seductive before, is nothing compared to Jesus; I find myself wanting to know Him more.

Another Christian walking in the light is the last thing Satan wants, and he'll hit you hard and often to keep you from turning to God. He attacks with accusation, trying to drown you in despair: "You're such a hypocrite; you're no Christian. Look at how many times you've fallen. You've gone too far for God to love someone like you; you'll always be a sex addict." But 1 John 1:9 says:

If we confess our sins, He is faithful and righteous to forgive us our sins and to cleanse us from all unrighteousness.

There is no sin a Christian can commit that's bigger than the cross, and God's forgiveness, grace and cleansing are *always* available to you. When the deceiver hits you with accusation, you can turn to the Lord and say, "Father, thank you for cleansing me from all my sin by your blood at the cross; I ask that You fight the battle of these lies. Fill my mind and my heart with the power of Your truth so I can stand firm."

The forces of evil will try to increase your sense of isolation: "God's not here; do you see anyone? You're all alone. Did He help you when you masturbated with porn before? He's not going to listen to a sex addict like you." But Psalms 139:7–12 says:

Where can I go from Your Spirit? Or where can
I flee from Your presence? If I ascend to heaven, You are there;
If I make my bed in Sheol, behold, You are there. If I take the
wings of the dawn, If I dwell in the remotest part of the sea,
Even there Your hand will lead me, and Your right hand will
lay hold of me. If I say, "Surely the darkness will overwhelm
me, and the light around me will be night," Even the darkness
is not dark to You, and the night is as bright as the day.
Darkness and light are alike to You.

And 2 Chronicles 30:9 says:

For if you return to the Lord, your brothers and your
sons will find compassion before those who led them
captive and will return to this land. For the Lord your

God is gracious and compassionate, and will not turn
His face away from you if you return to Him.

God is all around you, no matter where you are or what you're doing. If it's 2:00 a.m. and you're getting tempted, He's right there, waiting for you to turn to Him. The evil one wants you to buy into the lie that God is far away and you're alone so you fall into despair and give in. But you can turn to the Lord, saying something like "Father, although I feel alone, I know you're all around me; You said You're everywhere, and I believe you. Fill me with Your presence now; fill this room with your peace. Be my strength and shield in the battle against despair and loneliness and be bigger to me than anything else."

The evil one also tries to get us to think we've sinned when we've not by attacking with the fear of sin: "You saw that girl and you lusted for her, you hypocrite! You've already sinned, so you might as well take the next step, get some porn, and have fun with it."

Every thought that flutters into your mind isn't sin, and just because an attractive person crosses your field of vision, it doesn't mean you've lusted after them. It's when we run after temptation with a butterfly net that it turns to sin. The evil one tries to make you *think* you've sinned so you stumble on something that isn't there. But you can turn to the Lord, and say, "Father, you know the true motives of my heart. If I have sinned, I invite you to convict me. However, I believe I'm being attacked with lies and accusation, so I ask you to fight the battle for me and fill me with the truth."

We will know by this that we are of the truth, and will assure
our heart before Him in whatever our heart condemns us; for
God is greater than our heart and knows all things.

1 John 3:19–20

You can detect an attack of fear if an overwhelming wave of terror washes over you.

In my experience, the Lord lets us know we're on the wrong path with a sharp sense of conviction or restraint from within, not a blast of fear.

For God has not given us a spirit of timidity (fear),
but of power and love and discipline.

2 TIMOTHY 1:7

If you're hit with fear, you can turn to God and say something like, "Lord, Your word says You haven't given me a spirit of fear, and I won't back down because you're bigger than the one who's attacking me. Please take the battle in your hands and fight for me."

Learning a new habit takes consistent effort and hard work, and making turn and connect a way of life is no different. As a teenager, when I first started working out with weights I would get exhausted quickly; I had little muscle development and no endurance. I kept at it and have now been working out with weights three to four times a week for the past 25 years. Today I'm in much better shape and can lift a lot more than I could in my teens; I also have few health problems.

It's the same with building up our spiritual muscles. In the beginning it will take a lot of effort to turn to the Lord every time you get hit; you may find yourself needing to turn to God many times every hour. Some battles last longer than others, and you need to build up endurance. When I was in the salon, I had to stay connected with Lord the entire time I was there. You might get discouraged and feel like it's too much work; soon you hear the Snake from Hell whispering, "It would be easier if you just gave in; remember how good it feels to masturbate? Wouldn't it be a relief to get this over with? You wouldn't have to fight any more." This is Satan's battle strategy to try to keep you in bondage to sin; don't give in. If the weight gets too heavy and you need a spotter, get on the phone immediately and ask your brother for help.

Lust softens spiritual and mental muscle, and it takes time to build it back up. Be patient, persistent and realistic; don't expect to bench 300 pounds one week after you start. In time you'll find that you're turning to God by habit, and temptation won't scare you like it used to. One day you'll notice that your bench press has gone up 25%; you'd been so focused on the battle that you hadn't paid attention to the improvements taking place.

There have been a few times when I've turned to the Lord and the thoughts and temptations kept coming; the cause was always unresolved sin in my life. Often, it was because I'd been unkind to my wife and our relationship had drifted apart. A disconnected marriage is an open door for spiritual attack, so keep short accounts with your spouse. If you've hurt your wife (or another person), make it right quickly.

Be of sober spirit, be on the alert. Your adversary, the devil, prowls around like a roaring lion, seeking someone to devour.

1 PETER 5:8

A big mistake many guys make is that they let up after getting a little freedom from sexual sin. We live in a cultural cesspool of pornography and sexual depravity, and Satan's brewing bigger vats of sewage. A few weeks, months or even years will not make you immune to temptation. Remember, David fell to adultery with Bathsheba in an unguarded moment after incredible success, which included defeating nine-foot Goliath in one-on-one combat, victory in many bloody battles, and becoming king. Peter denied Christ after having been involved in a lot of powerful ministry. It's easy to start thinking we're strong enough to handle temptation on our own and become complacent; don't make that mistake.

Establish my footsteps in Your word,
and do not let any iniquity have dominion over me.

PSALMS 119:133

I start every day by asking the Lord to "let no lust, fear or pride have dominion over me." Like David and Peter, I'm stuck with this vessel of broken flesh until death. Although the Lord set me free from the bondage to sexual sin in 1999, turn and connect must be my way of life, every day, as I showed in the story of when I bought the gift certificate.

I add fear to my Psalms 119:133 request because I've struggled with it as a result of abuse issues growing up. God has rebuilt this part of my life and for the most part I live free from fear and anxiety, but it's a soft spot I still have to watch out for.

Pride is a subtle snake that's always lurking at the door of my life, trying to quench God's spirit and thwart His work through exaltation of self, so it's added to my morning request. It's easy to watch God change lives and then get hit with thoughts wanting praise for what He did. When I hear the snake of pride hissing, I turn to God: "Lord, please don't let my pride take hold here, the glory is Yours, not mine; Your grace is sufficient for me. Please help me so that I don't get in your way or charge ahead of you; I want to follow You."

Finally, brethren, whatever is true, whatever is honorable,
whatever is right, whatever is pure, whatever is lovely,
whatever is of good repute, if there is any excellence
and if anything worthy of praise, dwell on these things.

PHILIPPIANS 4:8

The verse above shows what we should dwell on; He has given us many things that are "lovely, of good repute, excellent, and worthy of praise." Saturate your mind in God's word every day, filling it with all of His truth and blessings.

Take in the refreshing sights of His beaches, deserts, mountains, forests, and meadows. Get out of your office with its flickering lights, demands on time and pale white walls, and breathe in the refreshing beauty of God's creation. Learn to enjoy the sounds around you, such as the rhapsody of crashing waves, the melody of a bird, the soft drumbeat of rain, and the laughter of children.

Music is a gift that can minister to the hardest heart; Saul was soothed from an evil spirit when David played the harp (1 Samuel 16:23). Immerse your mind in music that worships Him; let your soul dance with an uplifting chorus that soars to Heaven, or find peace in a quiet instrumental.

We should avoid music with sexually suggestive or angry lyrics; this can turn us back to lust as quickly as the right music takes us to the throne of Heaven.

Let your mind find peace by discovering the healing mystery of silence; make getting away from the messages and noise of this world a habit. Get alone with God; find a quiet meadow, go somewhere deep in a forest, take a walk in the desert, or find an empty room in your home early in the morning. Take time to quiet the ever-racing thoughts of your mind, and learn the secret of silent communion with the Living God; it will produce depth and stability in you that few Christians possess.

As turn and connect becomes your way of life, the Lord will change you. Your focus will evolve from self-absorption to God-obsession, and you'll turn to Him for everything. You'll find yourself praising Him more, and caring less about yourself. Your faith will grow from mustard seed to mountain as He becomes bigger to you than sin or temptation.

You're in the ring with Mike Tyson again, who's grinning, showing that gold tooth. He's standing, waiting for you to charge him in panic like before, but this time you look up and say, "Lord, this fight is too much for me; You take care of it."

Instantly, a large fist from Heaven smashes Tyson to the floor, completely obliterating him. You walk away, silently praising God for the victory.

How blessed is the man who does not walk in the counsel
of the wicked, nor stand in the path of sinners, nor sit in the
seat of scoffers! But his delight is in the law of the Lord,
and in His law he meditates day and night.
He will be like a tree firmly planted by streams of water,
which yields its fruit in its season and its leaf does not wither;
and in whatever he does, he prospers.

PSALMS 1:1–3

chapter six

Myyyyy Precioussss

~

"ALL THE 'GREAT SECRETS' UNDER THE MOUNTAINS HAD TURNED
OUT TO BE JUST EMPTY NIGHT: THERE WAS NOTHING MORE TO FIND
OUT, NOTHING WORTH DOING, ONLY NASTY FURTIVE EATING AND
RESENTFUL REMEMBERING. GOLLUM WAS ALTOGETHER WRETCHED.
HE HATED THE DARK, AND HE HATED LIGHT MORE: HE HATED
EVERYTHING, AND THE RING MOST OF ALL."

"WHAT DO YOU MEAN?" SAID FRODO. "SURELY THE RING WAS HIS
PRECIOUS AND THE ONLY THING HE CARED FOR? BUT IF HE HATED
IT, WHY DIDN'T HE GET RID OF IT, OR GO AWAY AND LEAVE IT?"

"YOU OUGHT TO BEGIN TO UNDERSTAND, FRODO, AFTER ALL
YOU HAVE HEARD," SAID GANDALF. "HE HATED IT AND LOVED IT,
AS HE HATED AND LOVED HIMSELF. HE COULD NOT GET RID OF IT.
HE HAD NO WILL LEFT IN THE MATTER."[1]

From the book The Fellowship of the Ring

In the opening minutes of *The Return of the King*,[2] the last
of the Lord of the Rings movies, the tale is told of how
Sméagol, a normal, beer-loving hobbit, came to be the twist-

ed, shriveled-up waif known as Gollum. A hobbit, for those unfamiliar with Tolkien's tale, is a stout, elf-like person that stands half the height of a full grown man.

As the movie begins, Sméagol is river fishing in a boat with his cousin Deagol, when a big fish hits Deagol's line and pulls him overboard. While floundering underwater, Deagol spots a shimmering gold ring at the bottom of the riverbed, grabs it, and surfaces. Upon seeing the ring in his cousin's hand, Sméagol is immediately entranced by it; and asks Deagol to give it to him "for his birthday present." Deagol refuses, and the two friends fight over the ring, with the end result that Sméagol strangles his cousin to death.

The ring that cost Deagol his life was one of power and enchantment, as Tolkien describes:

> *And much of the strength and will of Sauron passed into that One Ring; for the power of the Elven Rings was very great, and that which should govern them must be a thing of surpassing potency; and Sauron forged it in the Mountain of Fire in the Land of Shadow. And while he wore the One Ring he could perceive all the things that were done by means of the lesser rings, and he could see and govern the very thoughts of those that wore them.*[3]

Sauron was the dark lord who sought to rule all of middle earth, and it was the One Ring that Smeagol killed his cousin for. Enchanted by its power and wanting to keep it to himself, Smeagol leaves everyone he knows and retreats alone to the Misty Mountains. His new home is now a dark, cold, damp cave; quite a departure from the countryside cottages that normal Hobbits live in.

But merry times with hearty beer and good friends no longer matter to Sméagol. His diet is now raw fish, and he shrivels up physically, losing most of his teeth and all but a few strands of his hair. His voice becomes a raspy hiss and he rarely smiles, except when he's caressing his "precious," the name he gives the ring. In isolation, Sméagol's personality contorts and splits in two; he talks to himself incessantly, even later when he's forced to be around others. The once happy, well-adjusted hobbit is now known as Gollum, from the harsh, choking sound he makes when swallowing.

Like Gollum, today there are many Christians who are obsessed with a different kind of ring. They're as fond of their precious as Gollum was of his, and they retreat often into a cave of isolation to be alone with it.

And, like Gollum, they don't see what it's doing to them…

In his book *The Sexual Man*,[4] Dr. Archibald Hart surveyed some 600 Christian men on the subject of masturbation. Of those who were married, 61% said they masturbated, with 82% of these confessing they had sex with themselves once a week. Of the single men who responded under the age of 20, 96% admitted to a masturbation habit.

Since so many Christian men are having sex with themselves you'd think it was because they liked it, but in Dr. Hart's survey only 23% gave "enjoyment" as their reason for doing it. The rest said they masturbated "from habit," "because of their sex drive," "they were addicted to it" or "from lack of an outlet for sex."

In a weird twist reminiscent of Gollum's split personality, only 13% said they thought masturbation was a normal act, yet 97% said they didn't feel guilty about it. How could this be? Is it possible there are many men who would rather do without self-sex but don't know how to stop? And yet, if so many normal Christian men are having sex with themselves is it really hurting anything? Is masturbation just a harmless act of physical release?

To know whether something is harmful we must look at how it affects the user and those around him. Of course, for spiritual truth we always look to God's word. We'll do both in this chapter, beginning with the effects of masturbation.

In her book *An Affair of the Mind*, Laurie Hall writes:

Sex was created to send us outward. The word intercourse means "communication, a connection between people." When we choose to make it our own, we are saying we don't want to be bothered with the hard work of communication; we're not interested in connecting with anyone but ourselves. We are the center of our own universe... When the focus of sex is self-bent and inward, there can be no spirit to spirit communion with the person we love. Instead... sex implodes a man, driving him further into himself... When we are self-absorbed in our sexuality we will be self-absorbed in every aspect of our daily lives. The wife of a man who is enslaved to masturbation will not only be shut out of his sexuality, she will also be shut out of daily decisions and daily occurrences. He jealously guards it all for himself. He cannot afford to let anyone in. To do so would destroy his illusion of control.[5]

Laurie knew what she was talking about; her husband was a sex addict.

I had sex with myself from my teenage years until I was 36. (I was married at 26.) Like the others who responded to Dr. Hart's survey I couldn't have said enjoyment was why I masturbated; I always felt empty after the act was over, and there was always a sense that something was missing. As Laurie wrote, sex is about connection and communication with another; spirit-to-spirit communion with the person we love. When I masturbated there was no bonding with another in warmth, intimacy and love; instead, I was "connecting with myself," causing a bizarre emotional misfire that warped my character.

I tried to disconnect the spiritual from the physical, telling myself I needed masturbation just for physical release. After all, I reasoned, I should be able to have sex with myself as long as I'm not doing it with porn. But the emptiness, overwhelming sense of isolation, and shame were always there afterwards; porn or not. I couldn't talk myself into separating the emotional and spiritual elements of sex, anymore than Gollum could convince himself he had all his teeth.

Today I can see other ways masturbation affected me that I was blind to before.

I robbed my wife. Michelle wanted emotional and physical intimacy; two best friends taking a jog together, not me rushing ahead of her to the finish line. I deprived my wife of *me*; of my love and care for her. She wanted me to hold her, commune with her and cherish her, not use her for my personal pleasure machine.

Masturbation robbed us both of enjoyment. I didn't struggle with premature ejaculation as some do, but I could have pleased my wife a lot longer than I did. (Today after not having masturbated since 1998 it's different.) It's no accident when sex between a husband who masturbates and his wife is a short story; it's what he's trained himself to do.

Masturbation warped me emotionally. Opening up to Michelle on a deeper level was miserably hard; emotionally I was like a man with laryngitis trying to talk. I had spent so much time hiding in the Misty Mountains of my own misery and isolation that I had lost the ability to relate to others. Self-absorption traps a man deep inside of himself.

Like Gollum with the ring, my precious (sexual release) became my master. I was self and sex-absorbed, driven by physical urges and desires. If I couldn't have an orgasm when

I wanted it, I got angry, anxious or depressed. Sexual release was my god, comfort and love; the source of my life.

I think the fallout from masturbation that grieved me the most was the separation from God I experienced whenever I worshipped at the altar of self-sex. I knew Jesus had living water that could fill my soul, but I chose to "drink from myself" instead. I felt as far away from the Lord as I did from my wife and others.

Of course, the obvious problem with masturbation is that many men use it with pornography, and/or they run sexual fantasies in their mind during the act. This is plainly sin, as Jesus' words in Matthew 5:28 testify; using sex with self to enhance the experience of adultery in the heart. From my conversations with other men I know that masturbation accompanied by sexual fantasy and/or pornography is the norm, not the exception.

Let's now turn our attention to God's word and see what He says about masturbation. What I hear from many Christians is that having sex with themselves is okay because it's not specifically addressed in the Bible. But if "thou shalt not" is the standard for whether something is sin or harmful, we can smoke marijuana or abuse other drugs because there's no "thou shalt not smoke pot" in the Bible.

"Wait a minute!" you say. "It's obvious that smoking marijuana is a sin because the Bible prohibits drunkenness, and smoking pot clearly violates this principle!"

I agree; we need to look at the principles in God's word as well as the Thou Shalt Nots.

Principle #1: The only time when sex is sanctioned in God's word is in the context of a marriage between one man and one woman.

In Genesis 2 we read:

For this reason a man shall leave his father and his mother, and be joined to his wife; and they shall become one flesh.

Note the "two becoming one" emphasis on connection and communion between one man and his wife. Hebrews 13:4 adds:

Marriage is to be held in honor among all,
and the marriage bed is to be undefiled;
for fornicators and adulterers God will judge.

Here again, the marriage bed is the sole context given for God sanctioned sex.

Carefully, read this verse:

Yet I wish that all men were even as I myself am (single).
However, each man has his own gift from God, one in this
manner, and another in that. But I say to the unmarried and
to widows that it is good for them if they remain even as I.
But if they do not have self-control, let them marry;
for it is better to marry than to burn with passion.

1 CORINTHIANS 7:7–9

The door is wide open in this passage for masturbation to be shown as a viable, God-sanctioned alternative to marriage; after all, Paul was encouraging the Corinthian believers to be single. If he wanted them to have sex with themselves so they could avoid marriage, Paul would have written something like this: "But if they do not have self-control, let them masturbate or marry; for it is better to have sex with self or marry than to burn with passion."

But he didn't; marriage is the *only* outlet for sexual release provided in this verse, and, in fact, all of God's word.

The one man/one woman connection is developed again in the following verses:

Yet the body is not for sexual immorality, but for the Lord, and
the Lord is for the body. Do you not know that your bodies are
members of Christ? Shall I then take away the members of
Christ and make them members of a prostitute? May it never

be! Or do you not know that the one who joins himself
to a prostitute is one body with her? For He says, "The two
shall become one flesh." But the one who joins himself to the
Lord is one spirit with Him. Flee sexual immorality.
Every other sin that a man commits is outside the body,
but the sexually immoral man sins against his own body.
Or do you not know that your body is a temple of the Holy
Spirit who is in you, whom you have from God,
and that you are not your own? For you have been bought
with a price: therefore glorify God in your body.
1 CORINTHIANS 6:13B, 15–20

Sex is again shown in the context of "two becoming one flesh." Note also how "your bodies are members of Christ," "but the one who joins himself to the Lord is one spirit with Him," and "your body is a temple of the Holy Spirit," are woven in with the prohibitions against sexual sin, highlighting the spiritual element of sex. When a man takes his temple, where the Holy Spirit is residing, and "becomes one body with a prostitute" there is a profound negative impact on his spiritual life. Sex isn't merely a physical act.

Principle #2: Masturbation is never offered as a way to deal with depression or find comfort.

In 1 Kings 18, we read the well-known story of what happened when Elijah confronted the nation of Israel. Taking a huge step of faith and showing incredible courage, Elijah challenged the wicked king Ahab and the prophets of Baal to a fire duel, where the god that responded by burning up a sacrificed animal first would be the one the nation would follow. The Lord responded powerfully by torching Elijah's offering, and many of the prophets of Baal were killed. It was an amazing triumph.

However, in 1 Kings 19:2–5 we read:

Then Jezebel sent a messenger to Elijah, saying,
"So may the gods do to me and even more, if I do not make
your life as the life of one of them by tomorrow about
this time." And he was afraid and arose and ran
for his life and came to Beersheba, which belongs to Judah,
and left his servant there. But he himself went a day's
journey into the wilderness, and came and sat down
under a juniper tree; and he requested for himself that he
might die, and said, "It is enough; now, O Lord, take my life,
for I am not better than my fathers." He lay down and slept
under a juniper tree; and behold, there was an angel touching
him, and he said to him, "Arise, eat."

When Elijah fell into depression after Jezebel threatened to kill him, we don't read that he masturbated to comfort himself after arriving in Beersheba, nor do we read anywhere in Scripture where a person had sex with themselves when depressed. Masturbation isn't to be used for comfort, instead—

Principle #3: We are to receive our comfort from Christ.

…Who comforts us in all our affliction so that we will be able
to comfort those who are in any affliction with the comfort with
which we ourselves are comforted by God.

2 CORINTHIANS 1:4

I used masturbation many times as a way of coping with stress, fear or anxiety, but the "comfort" I received was always short lived, and accompanied by emptiness, shame, and a sense of separation from God. A four-second orgasm cannot fill emotional or spiritual needs. What I should have done was turn to Christ, Who is willing to comfort me in every situation. His comfort is *real*, and goes far deeper than anything masturbation can provide.

Principle #4: We are to be the master of our bodies and their accompanying urges; our flesh is not to rule over us.

But I discipline my body and make it my slave, so that, after I have preached to others, I myself will not be disqualified.

I CORINTHIANS 9:27

Beloved, I urge you as aliens and strangers to abstain from fleshly lusts which wage war against the soul.

1 PETER 2:11

All things are lawful for me, but not all things are profitable. All things are lawful for me, but I will not be mastered by anything.

1 CORINTHIANS 6:12

For this is the will of God, your sanctification; that is, that you abstain from sexual immorality; that each of you know how to possess his own vessel in sanctification and honor, not in lustful passion like the Gentiles who do not know God...

1 THESSALONIANS 4:3–5

We are to "discipline our body and make it our slaves." When masturbation was a part of my life, I was an obsessed, Gollum-like slave to my body and its urges. We are not to be mastered by *anything*, writes Paul. A man who can't say "no" to his own whims and desires reveals his character is soft, and a man with a weak heart will succumb easily to temptation.

Like a city that is broken into and without walls is a man who has no control over his spirit.

PROVERBS 25:28

Our culture bombards us with messages like "if it feels good, do it" and, "you deserve a break today." If you're sexually aroused, just feed the impulse, it won't hurt anything. Go ahead, have sex with yourself or anyone you want. You have needs, after all, and you're only human.

God's ways and our culture's messages are at war with each other. The world tells us to obey our urges while God tells us to master them. It's Instant Gratification versus Self Discipline; a passive man weakened from pleasure versus a strong man of character who can say no. "It's all about me" versus "I will have sex with no one but my wife;" Softheart versus Braveheart.

Let's stack up the scales for and against masturbation and see which side holds the most weight:

The Blessings of Masturbation	The Other Side of the Coin
It feels good for a few seconds.	The loneliness, emptiness, and shame last a lot longer than the fun part.
I can have an orgasm whenever I want.	Promotes the instant gratification ("all about me") way of life.
I can do it alone.	No connection, bonding or warmth with another person.
I don't need to please my wife.	The spouse is robbed emotionally and physically.
I can feed my sexual desires all I want.	Self-absorption and sex-obsession develops.

The Blessings of Masturbation	The Other Side of the Coin
I can deal with my urges when they hit.	Violates the principle in God's word that we are not to be mastered by our urges.
	Violates the "marriage only" context of God's word.
	Violates the "comfort from Christ" principle in God's word.
	Separation from God.
	Masturbation softens and warps the character.
	Masturbation is used as a false coping mechanism for dealing with life.
	Masturbation is often used with pornography and sexual fantasy, which is clearly sin.

What kind of Christian do you want to be?

When lust ruled my life and I'd hear of another Christian who'd made a bold stand for God, I often felt convicted; his strength and courage were a sharp contrast to my soft character. If I couldn't say no to my sexual whims, I knew I'd be too weak to make a real stand for Christ, especially with fierce opposition. I think most Christian men want to be a Braveheart who can stand strong in the midst of overwhelming opposition like Elijah; they want to rule their urges and desires.

1. First, let's be honest: stopping a habit like masturbation won't be easy, especially if it's been a lifelong obsession. Dealing with our sexuality doesn't mean we deny it, stuff it, or put on a phony Good Christian Who Never Gets Horny act. We are sexual beings, and it's not always easy to say no.

2. Put sex in its proper perspective. Sex isn't life, and it isn't love; it won't fill the emptiness in your heart, and it can't solve your problems. Solo ejaculation is a quick shot of pleasure that will leave you feeling more miserable, empty and lonely than you were before, for a much longer period of time; I remember having lust hangovers that would last for days, even weeks. You don't *need* sex, and you won't die without it. Sex was never meant to be a god.

3. Jesus is life: "I am the way, the truth and the life" (John 14:6), and only His love can touch the deepest, loneliest places of your heart. When sexual desire hits, remember that your deepest need is for God's life and love, not an orgasm. As we discussed in the last chapter, turn your focus away from the physical feelings and to the Lord, and ask Him to fill the emptiness in your heart with His love and life. Freely confess your weakness, and let Him fight for you. The burning will pass, as it always does.

4. If you get hit in the middle of the night with temptation, do something to break it up. If you're not wearing much, put on a little more clothing to help keep any feelings of

sensuality at bay. Open up God's Word, or turn on some praise music.

5. The first few months are always the toughest, and there may be times when you need help. If you get over-whelmed, get on the phone with a brother; it's amazing how this always cuts a Mt. Everest sized temptation down to size.

6. Be aware of situations going on behind the scenes that add to the battle, such as an inordinate amount of stress, unconfessed sin, or an unresolved relationship (especial-ly with your spouse). Do what you know you need to do now to resolve these issues.

7. Don't let failure get you down. Mistakes are teachers; learn from them, make adjustments and keep going. The forces of darkness love to pound us with thoughts of despair and hopelessness so they can keep us trapped in sin and shame; don't buy into it. Remember the cross.

8. Assuming there are no physical or medical issues to pre-vent it, you should be *vigorously* exercising several times a week, and I don't mean walking around the block. Personally, I like lifting weights, but what you do isn't as important as that you do it. Without exercise, stress builds up inside, making masturbation a tempting release valve. If I don't work out for a few days I feel like a full can of coke that's been shaken and ready to explode; our bodies need exercise to blow off the steam that builds up from the pressure of life.

9. Eating too many "comfort foods" (ice cream, sweets and salty snacks) is using food for pleasure, and can be a door-way for sensuality. Limit your intake of these foods, and keep your diet balanced.

Every marriage goes through a period of time where sex is put on hold, which means we will need to cope with celibacy in marriage. My wife was pregnant three times from 1999 through 2004. After the fifth month of pregnancy she doesn't want sex; it's physically uncomfortable for her, and she gets self-conscious about her changing appearance. Counting recovery time from three C-sections, this means I had about 21 months of marital celibacy in five years. I had three choices as to how I could have dealt with this:

1. Masturbate (not going to happen).

2. I could have pulled out 1 Corinthians 7:5 and shot her with "stop depriving one another" in the hope of manipulating her with a guilt trip. We still wouldn't have had sex, and I would have driven us further apart; I would have been stuck in bitterness for what I couldn't have, and she would have resented me for not being more understanding of her situation. We both lose.

3. I could choose death:

> *"Husbands, love your wives, just as Christ also*
> *loved the church and gave Himself up for her…"*
> EPHESIANS 5:25

In marriage, there will be times when we need to crucify our right to sex for a little while. Death is painful, and putting what we want up on the cross is neither easy nor pleasant. To sleep next to the one woman in the universe I could have sex with and hold back for a number of months was hard. There were times when I found myself pulling away from her emotionally, and had to remind myself that (1) our marriage wasn't just about sex, (2) Michelle was my best friend, and (3) she was going through a lot of physical discomfort. My clay-pot weakness kept me on my knees drawing strength from the Lord, and I continued to share my struggles with my brothers, who would bless me by praying for my wife and me.

As all things come to an end so did our period of marital celibacy. Because I didn't masturbate, I was able to come back to my wife with confidence, knowing I hadn't been setting our marriage up for more problems. Lust always wants more, and masturbating would have opened up the door of temptation for me to use porn to spice it up. I had no desire to live in a cave in the Misty Mountains of isolation again, so self-sex wasn't an option.

I am not saying a wife should purposely withhold sex from her husband or that he should passively say "okay" if she does. Marriage is the one place where the flames of sexual desire should be fanned into a glorious bonfire; they should *never* be intentionally snuffed out. The point is that there will be times when your wife will go through emotional hardship, or physical difficulties, and you will both be blessed if you show her grace, understanding, and love instead of demanding your due.

Picture a church filled with an army of Braveheart Christian men who say no to instant gratification and self-centeredness. They model strength, transparency, and integrity to their families, and love their wives as Christ called them to. If God calls them to stand firm in battle, they're ready. This is the standard we're challenged to aspire to.

Or, you could hobble around hissing "the precioussss... I need the preciousss..."

chapter seven

The Morning After

~

MY SON, GIVE ATTENTION TO MY WISDOM, INCLINE YOUR EAR
TO MY UNDERSTANDING; THAT YOU MAY OBSERVE DISCRETION
AND YOUR LIPS MAY RESERVE KNOWLEDGE. FOR THE LIPS
OF AN ADULTERESS DRIP HONEY AND SMOOTHER THAN OIL
IS HER SPEECH; BUT IN THE END SHE IS BITTER AS WORMWOOD,
SHARP AS A TWO-EDGED SWORD. HER FEET GO DOWN TO
DEATH, HER STEPS TAKE HOLD OF SHEOL. SHE DOES NOT
PONDER THE PATH OF LIFE; HER WAYS ARE UNSTABLE,
SHE DOES NOT KNOW IT.

Proverbs 5:1–6

A little lust won't hurt anyone" is one of Satan's greatest lies. However, the man who has given himself over to sexual sin doesn't realize he's soaking *all* of his heart in evil. Blinded by darkness and corruption, he cares only about himself and what he wants; God and others matter only when he needs them. As his pride swells, lying, stealing, cheating and compromise spread into every area of his life.

The prophet Isaiah provides a picture of those who are lost in the darkness of sin:

We hope for light, but behold, darkness, for brightness,
but we walk in gloom. We grope along the wall like
blind men, we grope like those who have no eyes;
we stumble at midday as in the twilight, among those
who are vigorous we are like dead men. All of us growl
like bears, and moan sadly like doves; we hope for justice,
but there is none, for salvation, but it is far from us.
For our transgressions are multiplied before You, and our
sins testify against us; for our transgressions are with us, and
we know our iniquities: transgressing and denying the Lord,
and turning away from our God, Speaking oppression and
revolt, Conceiving in and uttering from the heart lying words.

ISAIAH 59:9B–13

Slavery to sexual sin "multiplies transgressions," and no sin burns faster through the field of the heart than "lying words." The man who's living a lie (I'm a good Christian who would never touch porn) must hide his porn/sex addiction (lie #2) and lie again once his wife asks what he's doing. He becomes skilled in the art of "conceiving in and uttering lying words in his heart;" able to craft a convincing fib at a moment's notice.

One wife told me that when she walked in on her husband as he was watching porn on their TV at 2:00 in the morning, his response was, "Uhhh, I was channel surfing and accidentally ran into the Playboy channel." In time, lying becomes so ingrained that it's harder to tell the truth than lie.

The husband who lies and cheats on his wife with porn or affairs will be dishonest at work and church as well. If he steals from the family bank account to buy porn at home, it won't be long before he'll embezzle time or money from his employer. An angry but proud Christian sex addict who refuses to take responsibility for how he's hurt his wife and kids will deflect attention to his co-workers at the office when confronted with a mistake he made there.

The tragedy in all of this is that his loved ones get hurt while a sex addict is in Multiplication of Transgression mode. When I woke up after my long dark night of corruption and sexual sin and saw the trail of wreckage I'd created, it made me sick.

I broke up a family.

When I was 21 and single, I had an affair with a married mother of three children that lasted for three years. Her husband was a friend of mine from work who invited me to live in their home. In my hunt for sex I didn't care who I hurt; all that mattered was what I wanted. Their marriage ended in divorce, leaving my friend's wife a single parent of three fatherless children.

As a Christian, I financed the sex industry.

Every time I had sex with a prostitute or acted out with porn, I was abusing someone's daughter. Shelley Lubben, a former porn actress and prostitute who is now a strong Christian who ministers to others in the sex industry, writes:

I was more apt to spend time with Jack Daniels than some of the studs I was paid to "fake it" with… none of us like doing porn. In fact, we hate it. We hate being touched by strangers who care nothing about us. We hate being degraded with their foul smells and sweaty bodies. Some women hate it so much you can hear them vomiting in the bathroom between scenes. Others can be found outside smoking an endless chain of Marlboro Lights…

…When we were little girls we wanted to play with dollies and be mommies, not have big scary men get on top of us. The same horrible violations we experienced then, we relive as we perform our tricks for you in front of the camera. And we hate every minute of it. We're traumatized little girls

living on antidepressants, drugs and alcohol; acting out our pain in front of YOU who continue to abuse us.

As we continue to traumatize ourselves by making more adult films, we use more and more drugs and alcohol. We live in constant fear of catching AIDS and sexually trans-mitted diseases. Every time there's an HIV scare we race to the nearest clinic for an emergency checkup. Pornographers insist giving viewers the fantasy sex they demand all the while sacrificing the very ones who make it happen. In other words, no condoms allowed. Herpes, gonorrhea, syphilis, chlamydia, and other diseases are the normal anxieties we walk around with daily. We get tested monthly but we know testing isn't prevention. Besides worrying about catching diseases from porn sex, there are other harmful activities we engage in that are also very dangerous. Some of us have had physical tearing and damage to internal body parts."[1]

Every time I downloaded porn or rented a movie, I, a Christian, was funding and encouraging the rape and abuse of women in the porn industry. Sadly, the church may be one of the sex industry's biggest customers. In her book *Sex, Lies and the Media*, Eva Marie Everson recounts the following story:

My friend Jack Samad (with the National Coalition for the Protection of Children and Families) shocked me with the story of his attendance at a religious convention. The manager of the hotel where he had been staying noticed the posters and other paraphernalia he had carried through the lobby early one morning and then back in again later that afternoon. He stopped Jack and asked him what he was doing with all that information on pornogra-phy. Jack told him he was part of the Christian conference being held in the city. The manager chuckled. "Get real," he said. Porn movies in our hotel are accessed at a higher rate during Christian conventions than at any other time.[2]

I stole from my employer.

From 1981 through 1990, I worked at a company that sold machine shop supplies. During this time, I stole my employer's time by watching a porn movie in an X-rated theater during working hours. One afternoon (when I supposed to making sales calls), I raced home to my condo to have sex with the married woman I was having the affair with. Phone calls with women during company time, coming in late because of a hangover, and other distractions drained my productivity even more. Then, when I quit, I printed a customer list at the office and took it home. I used this list later when I started my own business.

I was blinded by pride, and cheated my customers.

In 1996, six years after I'd started my own business selling machine shop products, I decided to go outside my area of expertise (which was sales and marketing) and start a machine shop. I wanted to build a large company that many would be in awe of, a monument to Mike.

A year and several hundred thousand dollars of debt later, it was a disaster. The machine shop lost money every month, and was dragging the company down. I contacted a vendor of mine (who was also a friend) and asked if he would consider buying the more than $250,000.00 worth of machinery and inventory of the machine shop. In exchange, I agreed to make $40,000.00 of sales a month for him of the product I'd set the shop up to make, on a commission basis.

He bought the equipment, but I made little effort to carry out my end of the bargain.

I hurt Michelle deeply.

My adultery with porn and a prostitute shredded my wife's heart, and that was just the beginning. Lust hardens a man's heart and cripples him emotionally, so when Michelle would try to be affectionate I'd push her away. I wanted lust, not love. A man with a hard heart is a critical man, and I often made negative remarks about the way she did things, even if she'd done nothing wrong. She suffered with my rejection, cold heartedness and betrayal for most of the first 10 years of our marriage.

I wounded my kids.

On Christmas day 1998, about a month before God broke me (as was discussed in chapter four), Michelle videotaped our then family of four as we were opening presents. A few weeks later, we sat down to watch it.

In one scene my four-year-old son is seen ripping open a present. Bursting with joy, he turns to me to show off his new toy and says, "Dad, look what I got!" Although I'm sitting a few feet away, I don't reply; I'm engrossed in looking at something and it appears I don't hear him. "Dad... Dad... Dad!!!" he calls out again. I still don't acknowledge him; the expression on my face is numb and blank.

"*DAD!!*" he cries again; this time, with hurt in his voice.

Michelle's voice breaks in from behind the camera: "*Mike! Sean's trying to get your attention!*"

I wanted to throw up; I was looking at a man who was so self-obsessed that he didn't hear his four-year-old son calling to him from point-blank range. The person on that tape—me—looked like he didn't care about anyone (other than himself). *Had I purposefully ignored Sean?* I could tell he was hurt by my cold response; did he question whether I loved him, or whether he mattered to me? God had put a mirror in front of my face, and the reflection staring back was painfully ugly.

With the exception of the affair I had as a single man, all of the above occurred while I was going to church every Sunday and professing my love for the Lord as a good Christian.

But prove yourselves doers of the word, and not merely hearers who delude themselves. For if anyone is a hearer of the word and not a doer, he is like a man who looks at his natural face in a mirror; for once he has looked at himself and gone away, he has immediately forgotten what kind of person he was.

JAMES 1:22–24

There's work to be done once we wake up from our dark night of sin. Your trail of wreckage will not look the same as mine, but there are probably some wounded souls left lying in the road. Let's look at what we need to do.

All lying must cease.

Do not lie to one another, since you laid aside the old self with its evil practices…

COLOSSIANS 3:9

Every lie corrupts a man's character a little more, until he resembles the father of lies more than his Father in Heaven.

You are of your father the devil, and you want to do the desires of your father. He was a murderer from the beginning, and does not stand in the truth because there is no truth in him. Whenever he speaks a lie, he speaks from his own nature, for he is a liar and the father of lies.

JOHN 8:44

Conversely, living a life of thorough honesty makes you more Godlike:

Then the Lord passed by in front of him and proclaimed, "The Lord, the Lord God, compassionate and gracious, slow to anger, and abounding in lovingkindness and truth…

EXODUS 34:6

97

Relationships are built on trust, and honesty is the cornerstone that sets the foundation. Without honesty, relationships don't last. This is why many wives are often more angry at their husband for lying than for committing adultery; *when a man lies, he breaks down the foundation of his marriage.*

If your wife asks if you masturbated with porn and you did, tell her the truth. Better not to complicate the issue with a lie. Your honesty gives her hope and a reason to stick with you; lying does not. If you mess up at work, own up to it. Don't try to divert attention or blame to another employee. If you're a pastor at a church and someone from your elder board asks how you've been doing with sexual purity, tell the truth. You're a man who serves the Living God of all truth; your life and ministry are in His hands.

One reason we lie is because we want to avoid the consequences, however:

> *...God is not mocked; for whatever a man sows, this he will also reap.*
>
> GALATIANS 6:7

You won't put off the consequences; just delay them—with the compounding interest that comes from having to tell additional lies to buy more time. It's far better to admit to a mistake the first time and be done with it, rather than carry a burden that's increasing in size and weight.

A half-truth is just as bad as a whole lie. After I committed adultery with a prostitute in 1991, Michelle insisted that I get an HIV test. Humiliated, I went to the local doctor's office and told them what I needed.

"Why are you getting an HIV test?" asked the nurse.

"Because my wife asked me to," I said, in a sarcastic tone.

"*Well*, why doesn't your wife get a test too?" replied the nurse, indignant at the injustice of my situation.

Her response would have been different, I'm sure, if I'd have told her why Michelle wanted me to get tested.

There can be no healing with dishonesty. If a patient is coughing up blood and lies when his doctor asks if he's still smoking three packs of cigarettes a day, it is the patient who loses, not the doctor. You will stay spiritually sick if you persist in lying; it's like trying to tell God you're not a sinner and don't need the cross.

Once we've set the cornerstone of honesty in place, we can move on to the next stage of rebuilding.

Confess your sins to God.

If we say that we have no sin, we are deceiving ourselves
and the truth is not in us. If we confess our sins,
He is faithful and righteous to forgive us our sins
and to cleanse us from all unrighteousness.

1 JOHN 1:8–9

It's hard to live a lie without hiding and lying to the Lord. Go before Him and confess all deception, as well as any sins you've committed against others. I suggest you also ask for knowledge of His will as to how He might want you to deal with any damage you've caused.

Confess your sins to your accountability group/partner.

Therefore, confess your sins to one another, and pray for one
another so that you may be healed. The effective prayer
of a righteous man can accomplish much.

JAMES 5:16

This will help galvanize your desire to be a man of integrity, and your brothers can provide you with input on any actions you might need to take. Ask them to pray for the rebuilding of your character into God's image, as well as for healing of the hearts of those you've hurt, such as your wife.

Be reconciled to those who you've hurt.

Therefore if you are presenting your offering at the altar,
and there remember that your brother has something
against you, leave your offering there before the altar
and go; first be reconciled to your brother,
and then come and present your offering.

MATTHEW 5:23–24

Although my old employer didn't know I'd taken his customer list, God did, and He weighed my heart down with conviction until I made it right. When the president of the company I'd taken the list from, Jerry, heard I'd started my business, he got angry and insisted I was using his "trade secrets" to compete against him. I thought Jerry's accusation was baseless, as I could have easily obtained the contact information for those customers in the yellow pages. We both got attorneys and started preparing for a battle in court.

During the months it took to get the wheels of justice turning, the Lord started weighing on my heart with conviction about the list I'd taken. I resisted by justifying my position that Jerry's customers were public knowledge, but this didn't matter to the Lord; in His eyes I'd stolen from Jerry. As the weeks passed, the Lord kept pressing in with His will, until I finally wore down and surrendered. It was time to approach Jerry and confess what I'd done.

The possible consequences scared me. Once I told Jerry I'd taken his customer list, he could shut down my business and sue for damages; I'd be at his mercy. We had a mortgage payment and bills to pay, and in 1992 the economy wasn't doing well so it was a bad time to be unemployed. My choice was clear: resist God's will and take my chances in court, or jump off the cliff of faith and trust the Lord with the consequences. Fighting the Living God didn't seem smart, so I jumped.

I met with Jerry and told him I'd taken the list, and to my surprise he was gracious. I ended up paying him a commission on my sales for a few years, but this was far better than going to court and hoping I didn't lose everything (which I knew the Lord could orchestrate, if He wanted to). Most importantly, I could sleep again at night without dreaming about customer lists and attorneys.

Eight years later, the Lord started convicting me about the way I'd handled the machine shop sale. I'd sold Jim several hundred thousand dollars of equipment based on my word that I'd make $40,000.00 of sales a month for him—and bailed out. It had been several years since I'd sold the machine shop, and I knew Jim wasn't happy about it. While I still had my company (which I sold in 1998), he'd told one of my employees on the phone that "Mike has liability for what he did."

Although I was nervous about the possible consequences of once again putting myself in a vulnerable position, I'd learned from my experience with Jerry that (1) the Lord would weigh my heart down until I obeyed, and (2) I had to trust Him with the outcome. I called Jim, who lived in Southern California, and asked if I could fly out there and meet him for lunch. A week later, we were seated across from each other at a restaurant.

"When I sold you the machine shop, I know I agreed to sell $40,000.00 worth of product a month for you... and I didn't. It was wrong, and I owe you an apology for the way I handled it. If you want me to compensate you financially somehow..."

"Forget it," Jim said. "I'm just glad you apologized, because it removes the bad feelings I've had about what happened."

I was amazed at the grace the Lord showed me through Jim, a man who wasn't a believer.

A few years after we were married, I asked Michelle if she thought I should offer an apology to the man whose wife I'd had an affair with. "Could you get hurt?" she asked. The guy was a Vietnam vet with a bad temper, so it was possible; he'd come after me and broke the door down at my house while I'd been away on a business trip when I was living with his wife. "Then don't do it," was her reply.

The Lord doesn't call us to make a face-to-face amends in every circumstance. Michelle is my wife and first priority, and I've found that He often speaks His will through her to me. The Lord never put a weight of conviction on my heart to contact this man after I talked with Michelle, so I let it go. I've prayed for him, his ex-wife and their children many times.

In the end, there's nothing a man can do to make up for committing adultery with another man's wife. What I stole, I can never repay. That's not to say that I wouldn't have apologized to him if the Lord wanted me to, but that the consequences of adultery are permanent.

So is the one who goes in to his neighbor's wife;
Whoever touches her will not go unpunished. Men do not despise a thief if he steals To satisfy himself when he is hungry; But when he is found, he must repay sevenfold; He must give all the substance of his house. The one who commits adultery with a woman is lacking sense; He who would destroy himself does it. Wounds and disgrace he will find, And his reproach will not be blotted out. For jealousy enrages a man, And he will not spare in the day of vengeance. He will not accept any ransom, Nor will he be satisfied though you give many gifts.

PROVERBS 6:29–35

As I've learned the hard way, when the Lord wants us to make amends for something we've done, He has no problem placing a weight of conviction so heavy on the heart that we have to obey if we want to sleep in peace. Conversely, there are times where confessing what we've done to Him and others is enough. It's always best to get the counsel of your spouse, support group/partner, and of course, the Lord, before contacting someone for a reconciliation that might cause more harm than good.

As for his ex-wife, for me to contact a woman who I'd had a sexual relationship with in the past and wasn't a believer could cause much more damage than good, not only to her but also to my present wife. Some doors should be left closed.

I ceased abusing the actors and actresses in the sex industry when I stopped watching, downloading and purchasing sexually explicit material. On the positive side, I have the joy of helping other Christians reconcile with these precious souls by helping them break free from their addiction to porn. In a recent broadcast of the Blazing Grace radio show, we challenged the church to make the sex industry a mission field; these lost ones need our evangelism efforts as much as those living in a far away country. Think of the impact we'd have on our culture if many porn actors and actresses started coming to Christ!

The rebuilding of my marriage began when I confessed my sins to Michelle, and continued with consistent action, (see chapter three). The third building block is love.

So husbands ought also to love their own wives
as their own bodies. He who loves his own wife loves himself.

EPHESIANS 5:28

Loving Michelle means listening, not fixing; giving, instead of always looking to take; receiving her love instead of rejecting it. I had to learn how to be her best friend all over again; it grieves me that I allowed my sexual addiction to choke our marriage for so many years. When we can, we go on dates to keep our relationship fresh. (The goal is once a month, but this doesn't always happen.) I open my heart to her and trust her with my feelings now, rather than hide. When I blow it, I do my best to say, "I was wrong" as quickly as possible so we don't start pulling apart. We pray together most nights. Today, I can honestly say that Michelle's my best friend, and I am hers. She's seen my ugly side and still loves me.

The healing process for a wife and marriage that's been stressed by adultery or porn addiction could easily fill up a book; I've addressed this in Appendix' A and B.

Part of the process of rebuilding my life has meant learning how to balance family, work and ministry. It'd be easy for me to get so caught up in ministry and trying to save the world that I lose my family; I don't want to be a father who spends so much of his energy at work that he's a distracted zero when he's home. When our firstborn son was a baby and I walked into a store with him, I'll never forget when an old gentleman saw us, and simply said "years of joy." Once these "years of joy" are gone, we can't get them back.

One of sexual sin's most insidious effects is that it sucks a man's time and attention away from his kids. We have to set our priorities in life and then order our time around it. My kids need my love, attention, and discipline, and I don't want to be a father who neglects them emotionally or sets them up for their own struggle with porn or sexual addiction. Once a month, I try to take all four of my kids out on a date so they have time alone with me. Each of them hears "I love you" and gets a hug from me at least once every day.

In the process of making an all-out commitment to honesty and reconciling with those we've hurt, changes start to occur. "It's all about me" is replaced with "I care about you." The thick wall of pride breaks down, and our heart's load is lifted. Something wonderful happens; we start enjoying our relationships with our loved ones again, and the sound of laughter is heard in the house.

chapter eight

Into the Valley

~

"MANY YEARS AGO I WAS DRIVEN TO THE CONCLUSION THAT THE TWO MAJOR CAUSES OF MOST EMOTIONAL PROBLEMS AMONG EVANGELICAL CHRISTIANS ARE THESE: THE FAILURE TO UNDERSTAND, RECEIVE, AND LIVE OUT GOD'S UNCONDITIONAL GRACE AND FORGIVENESS, AND THE FAILURE TO GIVE OUT THAT UNCONDITIONAL LOVE, FORGIVENESS AND GRACE TO OTHER PEOPLE."[1]

David Seamands from his book Healing for Damaged Emotions.

So far, our focus has been on how to deal with lust and sexual sin; we've cut off the top of the weed, now it's time to dig deep into the roots, and pull. Then, we'll replace it with something pure, powerful, and wonderful; a new "plant" that gives life instead of draining it. As Bruce Marshall wrote, "The young man who rings the bell at the brothel is unconsciously looking for God."[2] If we do not find the God we're looking for, eventually we'll go back to the brothel.

In the eighth chapter of John, we find one of the most powerful and controversial stories in all of Scripture:

*Early in the morning He came again into the temple,
and all the people were coming to Him; and He sat down and
began to teach them. The scribes and the Pharisees brought a
woman caught in adultery, and having set her in the center
of the court, they said to Him, "Teacher, this woman has been
caught in adultery, in the very act. Now in the Law Moses
commanded us to stone such women; what then do You say?"
They were saying this, testing Him, so that they might have
grounds for accusing Him. But Jesus stooped down and with
His finger wrote on the ground. But when they persisted in
asking Him, He straightened up, and said to them, "He who is
without sin among you, let him be the first to throw a stone at
her." Again He stooped down and wrote on the ground.
When they heard it, they began to go out one by one, beginning
with the older ones, and He was left alone, and the woman,
where she was, in the center of the court. Straightening up,
Jesus said to her, "Woman, where are they? Did no one
condemn you?" She said, "No one, Lord." And Jesus said,
"I do not condemn you, either. Go. From now on sin no more."*

JOHN 8:2–11

For those who live in the condemning and damning world
of sexual lust, the words "from now on, sin no more" hit hard
and are often discouraging. No matter how hard I tried or
what I did, I could not "sin no more."

For years I was disheartened, but today, I know that my
problem was that I was trying to put icing on a cake that
hadn't been made.

Before He said "go and sin no more," Jesus said "I do not
condemn you"… to an adulteress… who'd been caught having sex with a married man not her husband, a crime punish-
able by death.

Why did He do this? Shouldn't He at least have waited
until she'd confessed her sin? Perhaps she did. When her

accusers said "Teacher, this woman has been caught in adultery, in the very act" she didn't deny it, nor did she defend her actions. Her silence alone was an admission of guilt. In addition, she might have already been convicted in her heart, something that only Jesus could see and know. Perhaps a look passed between Jesus and this woman—eye to eye—in which she *knew* that He *knew* the truth about her.

During those seconds with the Son of God, I believe she came to know Him, and received the power to live free from sexual sin. Why? First, her response of "No one, Lord" indicated a realization of who Jesus was. Second, those who don't know Christ have neither the power nor the desire to "go and sin no more" (Ephesians 2:1); they're enjoying their roll in the mud of sin and depravity, not looking for a way out. Since the Lord had told the disciples not to "give what is holy to dogs, or throw your pearls before swine" in Matthew 7:6, I doubt if He would have wasted His kindness on her if she had no interest in turning to God.

When Jesus said "I do not condemn you," He was bestowing grace, kindness, and forgiveness on her; the choice was hers as to whether she received or rejected it. She was forgiven of a sin that should have cost her life, and the normal response for someone who's been forgiven such an enormous debt is overwhelming gratitude and love for God.

For this reason I say to you, her sins, which are many,
have been forgiven, for she loved much;
but he who is forgiven little, loves little.

LUKE 7:47

A man or woman whose heart is filled with the love of God has little desire for the counterfeits of God's grace like porn or lust. Before we can "go and sin no more," we must receive "I do not condemn you;" the power to overcome and live free from sexual sin comes from receiving the love of God in the heart.

> *Or do you think lightly of the riches of His kindness*
> *and tolerance and patience, not knowing that*
> *the kindness of God leads you to repentance?*
>
> ROMANS 2:4

> *If you love Me, you will keep My commandments.*
>
> JOHN 14:15

A Christian sex addict is someone who hasn't received God's love in their heart. I have yet to talk to a man or woman who struggles with sexual sin who understands and has received God's grace. Often, they're just as lost and confused as I was. In my search for freedom from sexual sin, I spent nearly 13 years in counseling (seeing five psychologists and two psychiatrists along the way), more than eight years in the 12-step groups, and read plenty of books. Although I learned a lot, today I wish someone would have sat me down in the beginning, and said something like this, "Mike, in spite of all your knowledge and time in church, you've never received God's love; you're starved for it. You've spent years trying to find it in sex, work, drugs, people, and trying to 'be good enough' for God. The truth is that you don't really believe that God loves you in your heart. If you did, you wouldn't be a sex addict."

> *Just as the Father has loved Me,*
> *I have also loved you; abide in My love.*
>
> JOHN 15:9

> *But you, beloved, building yourselves up on*
> *your most holy faith, praying in the Holy Spirit,*
> *keep yourselves in the love of God, waiting anxiously*
> *for the mercy of our Lord Jesus Christ to eternal life.*
>
> JUDE 1:20–21

The word "abide" means to "remain in a place." We are to live in the love of God every moment of our life, regardless of failure or success. When we sin, we confess it (1 John 1:9), accept His forgiveness and grace, and move on, centered and secure in His love. There is no condemnation for those who are in Christ (Romans 8:1).

Let's revisit the first part of David Seamands' statement: "Many years ago, I was driven to the conclusion that the two major causes of most emotional problems among evangelical Christians are these: the failure to understand, receive, and live out God's unconditional grace and forgiveness...."

For many, the breakdown comes when they try to receive grace. They can't receive it, because they don't feel; they don't feel because they don't want to experience the pain and emptiness within. Since they don't want to experience what's really going on inside, they shut down, stuff, or avoid their emotions. They're so afraid of feeling that they wall off their heart, which keeps them empty; devoid of love, life, peace or joy.

God's Word gives us a picture of an empty Christian:

If I speak with the tongues of men and of angels, but do not have love, I have become a noisy gong or a clanging cymbal.

1 CORINTHIANS 13:1

I spent the first 36 years of my life in "gong mode." I didn't know how to receive love, and even if I did, I wouldn't have wanted to. Whenever someone would compliment me, show non-sexual affection, or give me a gift I would push it away; if I didn't decline it verbally, it was rejected internally. Love was a threat to my defenses; it stirred up feelings of hurt, yearning and anger, which I didn't want to deal with.

To keep others at arm's length, I carefully crafted a mask of success and wisdom so others would think I was self-sufficient. I was terrified that they might perceive me as weak or needy and might want to reach out and comfort me.

I tried to outrun my feelings by living at hyper-speed, but life is a marathon, not a sprint, and I'd eventually burn out. I couldn't stand quiet; when I'd go on a business trip and would be faced with the roaring silence of a hotel room, alone with nothing but my emotions, I'd turn to the TV for medication and recreation, hoping it would numb me. Watching TV led to porn and masturbation, which led to intense feelings of shame, and then more porn and masturbation, which hollowed out my love-starved soul even more.

When we shut our emotions down, all of them go, which means we forget how to lighten up and have fun. I stopped laughing and couldn't enjoy the simple things of life, such as sunsets at the beach, talking with my wife, or rocking my kids to sleep. My passion for basketball fell away, and porn became my only hobby.

My involvement in ministry was just as empty and loveless as I was, done for the approval and attention of God and men. My relationship with the Lord wasn't much better; I kept Him at a distance, just as I did with everyone else. My times in the morning with the Lord were a rushed ritual where I did most of the talking. I was afraid to listen for Him because I didn't want to hear what He might say; which I assumed would be anger, frustration or disappointment with my inability to "sin no more." A lot of my prayers were saturated with groveling and self-absorption; I was focused on my sin and how miserable I was, rather than on the Lord and what He wanted to give me. Grace is a gift that must be received, and I did everything I could to push it away.

For if by the transgression of the one, death reigned
through the one, much more those who receive the abundance

*of grace and of the gift of righteousness will reign
in life through the One, Jesus Christ.*

ROMANS 5:17

The pure water of "neither do I condemn you" has a hard time flowing through to a heart that's clogged with the silt of pain, lies, trauma, anger, fear, and/or rejection. If we want to experience all of the love, joy, peace, and love God has for us, we must descend into the dark valley of our heart and deal with the sin, lies, wounds, and distorted perceptions that keep us from receiving grace. The walls of deception and fear must be faced and torn down so the raw, tender places in the heart can be exposed to the light and healed. The process involves hard work and can be painful, but the end result is worth it.

Today, after having traveled through my own valley, I know there is no better way to live life. When sorrow and trials come, I hurt, grieve and sometimes cry, instead of attempting to run from, stuff, or spiritualize away what I'm going through. When I blow it or need help, I turn to God, ask for help or grace, and receive it, rather than turn to porn or some other counterfeit like lust. I've learned that silence is a blessing where I can receive blessings, love, direction, and even correction from the Lord. Living in God's love is infinitely better than wallowing in the lonely mud pit of porn, shame, self-absorption and emptiness.

*But I know you, that you do not have the
love of God in yourselves.*

JOHN 5:42

If we don't travel through the valley, temporary relief from sexual sin is the best we can hope for. Knowing what the Bible says about grace isn't enough; otherwise, none of those who attend Bible college or seminary would struggle with lust or any other type of sin. We must receive God's love from the heart; those who have allowed the surging river of His grace to flood the deepest recesses of their heart overflow in love for Him, in fulfillment of the greatest commandment:

Teacher, which is the great commandment in the Law?
And He said to him, "You shall love the Lord your God with all
your heart, and with all your soul, and with all your mind."
This is the great and foremost commandment.

MATTHEW 22:36–38

We cannot give what we have not received. As Seamands wrote, when Christians fail to receive God's love, they don't give that same unconditional love, forgiveness, and grace to others. A graceless and loveless church is cold, empty, and powerless; devoid of life or light.

The *last* thing Satan wants is to see a bunch of Christians fall in love with God; this is where they catch fire and become willing to live or die for Him, no matter what the cost. God's church shines like a blazing lighthouse of grace when it's filled with men and women who are passionate about the Lord, and it's this light that attracts the lost to Christ. I have yet to hear of a man, woman, or child who came to Christ because they were excited about being good, or spending hours studying the Bible. The deepest ache of man's heart is for God; to be filled with a life and love so powerful, bright, and holy that his heart glows with joy and peace.

As the deer pants for the water brooks,
so my soul pants for You, O God.

PSALMS 42:1

The oasis you're thirsty for is at the top of a mountain, across from the ridge we now stand. You can get there, if you're willing to descend into the valley that lies in between.

To get to the mountain we must go through the valley; there are no shortcuts, nor is there is a helicopter that can shoot us over to the other side. The valley is neither pleasant nor easy to travel; there are dark places within that cause even the strongest man to cower in fear.

The valley is not a place for those who want to fake it, or spiritualize their problems away. It's not for the legalistic, or the proud, or those who would pretend they have it all together. The valley is for men and women who are tired of playing church, and want the Real Thing. It's for those who aren't content with wading in the shallow end of the pool of life; they want every hindrance to receiving God's love and grace removed from their heart so they can live life to the fullest, experiencing everything the Lord has for them.

Examine me, O Lord, and try me;
Test my mind and my heart.

PSALMS 26:2

Test yourselves to see if you are in the faith; examine your-
selves! Or do you not recognize this about yourselves, that Jesus
Christ is in you—unless indeed you fail the test?

2 CORINTHIANS 13:5

The thief comes only to steal and kill and destroy; I came that
they may have life, and have it abundantly.

JOHN 10:10

chapter nine

Healing Father Wounds

~

A NEWSWEEK ARTICLE REPORTED THAT MIDDLE CLASS AMERICAN
FATHERS SPEND AN AVERAGE OF FIFTEEN TO TWENTY MINUTES PER
DAY WITH THEIR CHILDREN. IN MANY CASES, EVEN IF THE FATHERS
ARE PRESENT PHYSICALLY, THEY ARE ABSENT RELATIONALLY.
WE NEED MEN WHO WILL PLACE THEIR FAMILIES AS THE NUMBER
ONE PRIORITY IN THEIR LIVES. MEN WHO WILL GIVE AS MUCH OF
THEMSELVES TO THEIR CHILDREN AS THEY DO THEIR WORK.[1]

James Harnish

"IT'S CLEAR THAT MOST AMERICAN CHILDREN SUFFER
(FROM) TOO MUCH MOTHER AND TOO LITTLE FATHER."[2]

Gloria Steinem

"A CHILD IS NOT LIKELY TO FIND A FATHER IN GOD UNLESS
HE FINDS SOMETHING OF GOD IN HIS FATHER."[3]

Austin Sorensen

"WHEN A FATHER GIVES TO HIS SON, BOTH LAUGH;
WHEN A SON GIVES TO HIS FATHER, BOTH CRY."[4]

Jewish Proverb

In his book *Wild at Heart,*[5] John Eldredge writes:

A boy learns who he is and what he's got from a man, or the company of men... He cannot learn it from boys and he cannot learn it from the world of women. The plan from the beginning of time was that his father would lay the foundation for a young boy's heart and pass on to him that essential knowledge and confidence in his strength. Dad would be the first man in his life, and forever the most important man. Above all, he would answer the question for his son and give him his name. Throughout the history of man given to us in Scripture, it is the father who gives the blessing and thereby names the son.

"The question," Eldredge continues, is "*the* question, the one every boy and man is longing to ask. Do I have what it takes? Am I powerful? Until a man knows he's a man he will forever be trying to prove he is one, while at the same time shrink from anything that might reveal he is not. Most men live their lives haunted by the question, or crippled by the answer they've been given."

In their book *The Blessing*[6] Gary Smalley and John Trent describe the blessing Eldredge referred to not as a one-time event, but what every boy and girl needs from their parents growing up:

1. Meaningful touch; to be hugged consistently and often.
2. A spoken message; to hear the words "I love you" consistently and often.
3. Attaching high value; to know we matter and are worth being loved.
4. Picturing a special future, which is to know that we have potential—unique gifts and capabilities God can use to bless others with later on.

5. An active commitment, meaning we received the first four parts of the blessing on a consistent basis as we grew up. If a child hears his father say "I love you" once during the first 10 years of his life, he'll buy into the message of rejection from the silence of the nine years and 355 days, not what was said one time.

The reality is that many men—including those raised in Christian homes—grew up without "the blessing" or having their "question answered." The void that's left by the lack of our father's love is a setup for a long, hard struggle with sexual addiction, workaholism, gluttony or some other coping mechanism. Dr. Ross Campbell, a former associate clinical professor of psychiatry at the University of Tennessee College of Medicine, writes "in all my reading and experience I have never known of one sexually disorientated person who had a warm, loving and affectionate father."[7]

Neither have I. In our support groups I ask the guys to describe their relationships with their fathers, and I can't remember one man who said his father told him "I love you" and hugged him on a consistent basis growing up.

Scripture gives us several stories showing what happens when a man grows up with, or without, his father's love; Jacob's family being one of them.[8]

Now Israel loved Joseph more than all his sons, because he was the son of his old age; and he made him a varicolored tunic. His brothers saw that their father loved him more than all his brothers; and so they hated him and could not speak to him on friendly terms.

Genesis 37:3–4

When Jacob (who God gave the name of Israel) loved Joseph more than his brothers, he sent them a message that they weren't as deserving of their father's love as Joseph was.

How deeply this hurt them is evident in that they "hated him (Joseph) and could not speak to him on friendly terms." God's Word gives us insight as to how having (or not having) their father's love affected three of Jacob's sons when it came to sexual temptation: Reuben, Judah and Joseph.

Reuben

It came about while Israel was dwelling in that land, that Reuben went and lay with Bilhah his father's concubine, and Israel heard of it.

GENESIS 35:22

Judah

Now after a considerable time Shua's daughter, the wife of Judah, died; and when the time of mourning was ended, Judah went up to his sheepshearers at Timnah, he and his friend Hirah the Adullamite. It was told to Tamar, "Behold, your father-in-law is going up to Timnah to shear his sheep." So she removed her widow's garments and covered herself with a veil, and wrapped herself, and sat in the gateway of Enaim, which is on the road to Timnah; for she saw that Shelah had grown up, and she had not been given to him as a wife. When Judah saw her, he thought she was a harlot, for she had covered her face. So he turned aside to her by the road, and said, "Here now, let me come in to you"; for he did not know that she was his daughter-in-law.

GENESIS 38:12–16A

Joseph

It came about after these events that his master's wife looked with desire at Joseph, and she said, "Lie with me." But he refused and said to his master's wife, "Behold, with me here, my master does not concern himself with anything in the house, and he has put all that he owns in my charge. There is no one greater in this house than I, and he has

withheld nothing from me except you, because you are his wife.
How then could I do this great evil and sin against God?"
As she spoke to Joseph day after day, he did not listen to her
to lie beside her or be with her. Now it happened one day that
he went into the house to do his work, and none of the men
of the household was there inside. She caught him by his
garment, saying, "Lie with me!" And he left his garment
in her hand and fled, and went outside.

GENESIS 39:7–12

It can be no coincidence that Joseph, the man who was loved by his father, is the one who was able to say no to sexual temptation, while his brothers, who had "their question" answered differently, fell into it. It's likely that Reuben and Judah had a lifelong pattern of sexual sin; a man will not wake up one day and suddenly decide to have sex with his father's wife, or a prostitute.

Many of us had withdrawn, passive fathers who were there physically but missing in action emotionally. Eldredge writes: "Some fathers give a wound merely by their silence; they are present, yet absent to their sons… In the case of silent, passive, or absent fathers, the question goes unanswered. 'Do I have what it takes? Am I a man, Daddy?' Their silence is the answer: I don't know… I doubt it… you'll have to find out for yourself… probably not."[9]

Eldredge's father was around when he grew up; think of what happens when a family is ripped apart by divorce and a young child's father leaves. In spite of what their father may say or the time on the weekends he may spend with his kids, the roaring silence of Dad's missing presence during the week causes a child to think, "Did Dad leave because I didn't mean anything to him? … Surely he wouldn't have left if he loved me… I have must done something wrong… maybe I wasn't worth it to him." Their father's absence answers the question with, "You'll have to find out for yourself if you have what it takes… probably not, otherwise I would have stayed around. You weren't worth it."

For those who have been abused verbally, physically, or even sexually by their father, having a passive father would have been a blessing. The message of "You're a piece of worthless junk that no one could love" is violently pounded into them until receiving love and affection is almost impossible. How can I receive love if Dad, the "first and forever most important man in my life" says I'm a piece of worthless trash? Thus, porn or sex become the best and safest "love" I can hope for.

Brennan Manning sums up best what happens to a man or woman who grows up without their father's love and acceptance: "When a father's love is withheld, a child will struggle with issues ranging from shyness and insecurity to a profound and crippling shame over his or her very existence."[10]

Most guys try to fill the Grand Canyon sized hole in their heart from this "profound and crippling shame over their existence" with money, power, or sex. I tried all three. In my early 20's I discovered I had a knack for sales and marketing; I had no self esteem (which reveals how my "question" had been answered), so finding something I could do well was like throwing a bone to a starving street dog. I threw myself into my job full-force and charged up the company ladder, getting promoted to assistant sales manager, then national sales manager and, by the time I was 25, vice president of sales. The more I succeeded the emptier I felt, so I worked even harder, putting in six and seven-day workweeks and traveling as much as 40 weeks a year. Eventually I'd burn out and slow down, but letting off the throttle had the undesired effect of feeling the pain and emptiness I'd been running from, so it wouldn't be long before I kicked it into overdrive again. I spent years on the furious merry-go-round of work and burnout until God broke me of the idea that I could find love or acceptance from my success.

Not long after my wife and I were married in 1989, we went to see the movie *Dad* in a theater.[11] The movie tells the story of a workaholic father, Jake (played by Jack Lemmon), who is now retired, and his son John (played by Ted Dansen), who has followed in his father's footsteps. John has given his life to building up his career, sacrificing his first marriage and his relationship with his son along the way. Late in the movie, Jake goes through a life-threatening medical crisis and John visits his father in the hospital. Not knowing how long he has to live, Jake asks his son a question that hit me like a ton of bricks: "We've never hugged before... can we try now?" John hesitates at first, but he agrees, and father and son are seen embracing for the first time in their life.

Watching *Dad* was like running my heart run through a cheese grater for two hours, and as soon as we made it through the theater doors I broke down, sobbing uncontrollably. I ran to our truck, where my stunned wife held me for 10 minutes while I cried like a baby. Jake's story had hit the deepest nerve in my heart: I was the hard-charging, empty workaholic who was starved for his father's love and acceptance. The worst part was that I didn't know what to do about it.

My workaholic way of life poured gasoline on the fires of my struggle with sexual sin. Since I traveled a lot for business and couldn't say no to hotel porn, I was often going through the shame and emptiness from acting out sexually. I would "fix" my emptiness with more work, which left me emptier, so I needed more porn or sex to find comfort, and on it went, until I had a nervous breakdown in 1998.

Men who struggle with homosexuality have taken their father wound to a logical, albeit sinful conclusion. They may realize their need for masculine love more clearly than straight men do; however, a man can't soothe the wound in his heart by having sex with other men anymore than he can by having sex with women or masturbating to porn.

Father wounds are just as common in women as men, and little girls who were neglected growing up often end up marrying a man who is just like their daddy. In his book *Always Daddy's Girl*, H. Norman Wright shares the following about one of his female clients:

"I was amazed when another client, I'll call her Karen, described to me the kind of treatment she tolerated from men. She allowed them to mistreat her to the point of cruelty. She wasn't just a pleaser, she was a victim!

'I would like to find just one man who would treat me decently,' she said. 'I seem to be drawn to men who end up mistreating me, but I don't know why... what is happening to me?'

During the counseling process, Karen's lack of self-esteem became apparent. She carried deep wounds from the emotional abandonment she experienced as a child. Her parents' relationship was marked with anger and lack of fulfillment. Karen's father had little time for her, controlling her with his anger. There was no physical abuse, but plenty of emotional abuse. She felt worthless and insignificant, especially in her father's eyes.

Karen feels the same way as an adult. She anticipates and expects men to treat her as her father treated her. Karen seems to have an unconscious need to be a victim, which leads her to get involved with men who frighten her and abuse her."[12]

The reality is that most men who struggle with sexual sin were injured by their fathers growing up, and they married women with their own set of father wounds. This makes for a marriage fraught with pain and confusion, until both husband and wife take the time to look into the rejection that has so powerfully impacted their lives.

So what do we do with this deep wound within? Sex, alcohol, drugs, or money won't fix it, food can't comfort it (some use food, i.e., sensual eating, to try to fill up the hole in their soul), so the answer lies elsewhere.

First, pray.

Ask God to lead you in the process of healing.

Face the truth.

When I bring up father wound issues in our groups I often hear, "Well, my parents did the best they could." Defending our parents is a natural response born out of love, but it's also used to avoid facing the pain. We are hurt deepest by the people we love and need the most, and there is no deeper wound than the one that comes from our father. Evading or denial won't resolve a father wound; it must be faced.

Facing our father wound doesn't mean we blame our parents for the sin we used to medicate it. I chose sex and work to deal with my problems; my parents didn't force those decisions on me. No matter what our parents did, we must take 100% of the responsibility for our sinful choices.

Cultivate transparent relationships with other men.

We are wounded in our relationship with a man, our father, and it is in authentic relationships with other men where the healing process begins. Clean, non-sexual masculine love isn't found exclusively from our father. When our spiritual brothers accept and love us in spite of our faults, they unwittingly answer our question: "Yes, you have what it takes to be a man… you're important, and valuable, with gifts that bless me… I enjoy our friendship." Through their support and encouragement our brothers pass a blessing of masculine love and strength to us.

David was blessed this way by Jonathan, Saul's son. Read what David said after Jonathan was killed in battle:

> *I am distressed for you, my brother Jonathan;*
> *you have been very pleasant to me. Your love to me*
> *was more wonderful than the love of women.*

2 SAMUEL 1:26

David had several wives by the time he wrote this; he could have been satisfied physically by any number of women, yet his friendship with Jonathan was "more wonderful" than anything they could give him. Clean masculine love isn't complicated with sex or the emotional friction that arises from the differences between men and women. When another brother challenges me about an issue in my life, as long as it's done without an insult or cruel intent I can take it in stride. Men understand the fears and insecurities other men go through, so we can bless each other in ways that women can't. If I tell another man I struggle with lust, he can relate and help me. Telling a woman about my problems with sexual sin will be shaming for me (and perhaps embarrassing for her), and she'll have a harder time understanding.

Masculine love develops when we share our weaknesses and then allow our brothers to support, encourage, and, when necessary, correct us. My life is packed with other men; some I've met at support groups, others through work or church. Their acceptance of me, faults and all, is a resounding yes to my "question" that builds, encourages, strengthens, and blesses me.

Journal.

As you face the specific events that caused your wound, write them out in your journal to the Lord, expressing how your life has been affected by what happened. For example, if you had a passive father, write about the confusion and emptiness you've felt, and what you needed from your father. This will give voice to the cry of your heart and bring clarity to what you're going through.

During the process of journaling your emotions, the Lord may show you some issues that you need to deal with. Bitterness of heart often accompanies the pain of rejection, and the Lord could reveal the need to forgive your dad. Or you could see clearly for the first time how you've worshipped sexual sin as a false god, and the Lord could be inviting you to repent. If He brings an issue like this to the light, ask God how He wants you to deal with it, and take action.

We can't go back in time and recreate the father-son relationship we wanted, so grieving what was lost is a natural part of the process. Allow yourself to grieve what you didn't have with your father; doing so validates what you went through and provides an outlet for the pent-up emotion within.

Share.

As always, share what you're going through with the brothers in your accountability group. Show them what God has revealed to you, and ask them to pray for your healing in these specific areas. Bringing your brothers into the wound will be a soothing balm to your soul.

Write a letter.

Then, whether he's alive or not, write a letter to your father. In your letter you're going to share how you were wounded, forgive your father for what happened, and then bless him. Before you sit down to write, take a few days and pray first. This may be the most important letter you'll ever write, and you want God's hand in it. Ask the Lord to prepare your heart, and that you and your father will both be blessed through what you're about to write. Also ask that your father's heart is prepared to receive it.

Begin the letter by praising your father; what he's about to read won't be easy, so start on a positive tone. Then, express how you were hurt. Tell your father what you needed from him growing up; how you wanted to hear him tell you he loved you more often, or feel his touch, or how you wish you could have had more time together. Say this in a non-condemning way, without accusations or using phrases like "You should have…," or "If you had done this I would have had a better life." What's done is done, and the purpose of this letter is not to throw stones, but to heal. Tell the truth without using it as a sledgehammer to smash him with.

Then, forgive your father. Your forgiveness will cost you a lot, so don't write these words lightly; you're giving up your right to hold everything he did or didn't do against him for all time, with no turning back. Write your forgiveness simply and plainly, without a hint of expectation in your words of anything you might want in return.

After you've forgiven him in writing, express your love to your father. Tell him you accept him for who he is, past mistakes and all. Describe the things he did that you appreciate and what you love about him; build him up, and shower him with grace. You could also write an Old Testament style blessing to him; your father could be carrying a wound from *his* father, and this could be the first time in his life that anyone's ever blessed him. For ideas on how to write an Old Testament Blessing to your father, see Genesis 27:26–29, 28:3–4, chapters 48 and 49, and Number 6:23–24.

Once you've written the letter, take it before your accountability group, read it, and ask for their feedback. If they hear anything out of line, such as a condemning tone, make the appropriate changes and then read it again to them at the next meeting.

When the final draft is ready, have your brothers pray for you and your father. You pray first, by stating to the Lord that you are forgiving your father; ask that He prepares your father's heart and uses the letter to provide healing for both of you. Your group should follow up with more prayer for the same.

Before mailing the letter, seek your brothers' counsel about the timing. For example, if your father is going through a stressful time, or if he's having life-threatening physical problems it might be better to wait. (Or it could be that time is urgent and you need to send the letter overnight.)

After seeking the counsel of God and others, and once you feel the Lord is giving you the green light to mail the letter, send it. No matter how your father reacts, realize that you have no control over his response. Your healing isn't dependent on how he reacts, but in the freedom and peace you will discover by forgiving him.

If your father isn't alive, take heart; the expression of your soul's desires to your father can still provide healing to your soul. Brennan Manning tells the following story of a letter he had Rich Mullins write to Rich's father, who was deceased at the time he wrote it:

Seven months before he died, I guided Rich on a three-day silent retreat at Chateau Vineyard, a resort sixty miles north of Atlanta. He was in a state of emotional turmoil because of unresolved issues with his family of origin, specifically his father. Like Henry Nouwen's dad, John Mullins loved his son but never told him so. He was truly proud of Rich's accomplishments, shared his deep affection for him with other members of the family but failed to communicate his feelings to the one person who longed for his love...

During the retreat I asked Rich to write a letter to his deceased father. The next day I asked him to write a letter from his father to him. Rich resided in the chalet next to mine. As he wrote, I heard sobbing and wailing so loud that I started to cry myself. All John Mullins's pent up affection exploded and came cascading into Rich's heart like a torrent of truth and love. Soon after, Rich came to my place and read the letter, tears streaming down his face.

Next I asked Rich to write a letter to Abba followed by a letter from Abba to him. I shall never forget our festive dinner on the last night of the retreat. His black eyes shining like onyx and his face creased in a radiant smile, he said simply, "Brennan, I'm free."[13]

I hope by now you understand that we need other men in our lives to live the vigorous life of a Braveheart Christian. Like Rich, you can be free of the pain and rejection that's haunted your life. All you need is at least one other man who you can share with, the willingness to forgive, and God's hand in the process. Honesty with our weakness with the right men brings abundant blessings, not the shame and rejection we fear.

Resolving the wound left by the man who made the greatest impact in our lives is a critical part in our journey to grace, but it's not the final stop. Every human being is born with an empty chamber in their heart that can be filled only one way, by One Person. This chamber is set at the center core of the heart, and it's marked with a sign that reads, "For God alone." No person, thing, or experience has the ability to touch or fill this part of the heart.

Since the Living God is the only one who can fill an empty heart with life, light, love, joy, and peace, it is here in our journey where we turn toward His throne room.

chapter ten

Spring of Life or Concrete Block?

~~

THE HEART

"THE VITAL CENTER AND SOURCE OF ONE'S BEING, EMOTIONS,
AND SENSIBILITIES. THE REPOSITORY OF ONE'S DEEPEST
AND SINCEREST FEELINGS AND BELIEFS."

*The American Heritage® Dictionary
of the English Language, Fourth Edition*

"THE SEAT OF THE AFFECTIONS OR SENSIBILITIES,
COLLECTIVELY OR SEPARATELY, AS LOVE, HATE, JOY, GRIEF,
COURAGE, AND THE LIKE; RARELY, THE SEAT
OF THE UNDERSTANDING OR WILL;—USUALLY IN A GOOD SENSE,
WHEN NO EPITHET IS EXPRESSED; THE BETTER OR LOVELIER
PART OF OUR NATURE; THE SPRING OF ALL OUR ACTIONS
AND PURPOSES; THE SEAT OF MORAL LIFE AND CHARACTER;
THE MORAL AFFECTIONS AND CHARACTER ITSELF;
THE INDIVIDUAL DISPOSITION AND CHARACTER; AS, A GOOD,
TENDER, LOVING, BAD, HARD, OR SELFISH HEART."

Webster's Revised Unabridged Dictionary

Watch over your heart with all diligence,
for from it flows the springs of life.

PROVERBS 4:23

As in water face reflects face,
so the heart of man reflects man.

PROVERBS 27:19

A wise man's heart directs him toward the right,
but the foolish man's heart directs him toward the left.

ECCLESIASTES 10:2

I recently had lunch with a guy named Tom. A Christian for most of his life, Tom was married, the father of two children, and had been in an active ministry position in his church—until he voluntarily exposed his 18-year porn addiction to the leaders of his church... and his wife. Tom's life was in pieces.

After talking for a few minutes it became apparent that Tom was extremely insecure; he spoke at an almost manic pace, and apologized when he changed the subject (which was often). Tom admitted that he was hypersensitive to criticism, and to cope he'd mastered the fine art of manipulation and control. His marriage was under stress because he played a continuous game of cat and mouse with his wife in an attempt to avoid criticism at all costs.

Tom had learned how to say all the right words to impress others, especially in church settings. He had plenty of Bible knowledge, and enjoyed the approval and acceptance that came from being the "guy with the answers."

I asked Tom about his relationship with his father, and he revealed that his dad, a pastor, had been extremely harsh and critical of him during his childhood years. Tom's inability to measure up to his father's impossible standard of perfection had left him feeling unworthy and insecure.

"How do I stop the things I'm doing?" he asked. "How do I stop being so defensive, and how do I deal with this over-whelming insecurity?"

My answer was straight and to the point: "Accept God's grace."

Tom quickly changed the subject, and I knew I'd hit home. Eventually the topic of conversation turned back to God's love.

"Tom, growing up, you were brought up to believe that you had to be perfect for your father to love and accept you. But since perfection is impossible, deep down you bought into the idea that you couldn't be loved as you are. You've spent your life trying to be the perfect Christian in order to impress others and find acceptance, and you've bought into a lie that you have to be perfect for God to love you. All this time God has been holding out the big gift of His grace to you, but you've been saying 'I can't accept it; I'm not good enough.' Unlike your father, God sees how messed up you are, and accepts you, flaws and all. In spite of all the theology you know, you don't believe that God loves you."

Tom's eyes teared up, and his voice broke, "It's true, I don't even know *how* to accept God's love… I don't know how to get my arms around this…."

In his book *Breaking Free*, Russ Willingham, a former sex addict and counselor who now works with others struggling with sexual sin, writes: "I have yet to work with a sex addict, homosexual or troubled spouse who understands God's grace."[1]

After being around those who struggle with sexual sin since 1991, I know Russ is right. In our Strength in Numbers groups, the topic of grace is often what the men most want to discuss—and have the hardest time accepting. I'll never forget the look on a man's face one night as we talked about the story of the prodigal son. When we discussed the part where the father threw a party for his son's homecoming, one of the guys, with a pained look in his face, asked, "How do you imagine God throwing a party for you?" The idea that God would ever throw a bash for him was too painful for him to imagine.

Deep in their heart, those who struggle with sexual sin do not believe that God loves them. Their actions are proof of this, because the person who's had their heart filled with the love and peace of Christ has no desire for the sick counterfeit of lust. Those who turn to the sewer of sexual sin for love reveal they believe that "porn is as good as it gets for someone as worthless as me." No matter what they say, what ministry position they're in, or how much theology they know, if a man or woman turns to sexual sin they prove there is a dark place in their heart that's hidden from God's grace.

A common mistake we men make is that we "think our feelings"; we try to equate knowledge with belief. Webster's calls the mind "the intellectual or rational faculty in man; the understanding; the intellect; the power that conceives, judges, or reasons." The mind is an analytical processing machine, not the "spring of life." We don't experience the joy of love or the pain of rejection in our head—what man tells his wife, "I love you with all my head?" Many men "think their feelings" because they're afraid to face the pain within.

Read through these verses again:

> *Watch over your heart with all diligence,*
> *for from it flows the springs of life.*
> PROVERBS 4:23

> *As in water face reflects face,*
> *so the heart of man reflects man.*
> PROVERBS 27:19

> *A wise man's heart directs him toward the right,*
> *but the foolish man's heart directs him toward the left.*
> ECCLESIASTES 10:2

It is our heart—"the seat of moral life and character"—where our "deepest and sincerest feelings and beliefs" reside, that determines whether we "move to the right," like the wise man, or veer off to the left into sin. The beliefs in the heart determine if we can receive love from people and God or whether we will turn to lust.

You can process all the Scripture you want, but if your heart isn't able to accept the wonderful truths in God's Word, all your Bible study will have a boomerang effect. After the mind hears about God's grace, it analyzes it, computes "this is good," and then zips the message down to the heart. But the corruption from a virus of lies prevents the truth from getting through, and a "not worthy to receive" error is kicked back. Rather than looking into the heart, many try to fix the problem by resending the message or trying to process more truth.

How does a heart get infected with lies? Often our parents, who themselves may not have received God's grace in their heart, play a major role. Although some men experienced rejection from their mother, for many the roots lie in their relationship with their father. As Brennan Manning wrote, "When a father's love is withheld, a child will struggle with issues ranging from shyness and insecurity to a profound and crippling shame over his or her very existence."[2]

If the love we experience from others (especially the two people whose opinion mattered the most growing up) was conditional at best (or abusive at worst), the "springs of life" in the heart will be muddied with the lie that "this is what love is about." If we spend years polluting our heart with the shame from sexual sin, "porn is as good as it gets for me" as a way of life takes hold. Satan does his part by whispering, "You've sinned too much for God to love someone like you, look at what a hypocrite you are... God will never accept you until you clean up your life. You're hopeless, this is what you deserve." Eventually the heart dries up and resembles a concrete block instead of a spring of life.

The following are some of the lies many buy into:
1. I am worthless and defective.
2. Because I am worthless and defective, God doesn't love me.
3. I cannot be accepted as I am.
4. I must *do something* to earn God's love.
5. Sex, women, and/or porn can fulfill my emotional and spiritual needs.
6. I've sinned too much for God to forgive me.
7. If I am involved with ministry, or can abstain from sexual sin for long enough, God will love me.
8. God doesn't hear me; I'm on my own.
9. If I know enough of the right theology, I have accepted God's grace.
10. I can have a pure heart (true freedom from sexual sin) by something I do.

When a man is rejected, abandoned, neglected, or abused, the Father of Lies pours acid in the wound: "You're hopeless, fit only to be used by others; you'll never measure up; no one can love someone like you." In time, these lies set in the heart, and harden. When a man who struggles with "shyness and insecurity over his existence," like Tom, hears that God wants to throw a party for him, he can't accept it. He responds with apathy (it's hopeless, I can't have it), anger (enraged that others have what he can't), depression (anger turned inwards), or manic busyness (to avoid the pain of the core message of his life). It's like telling a parched, sunburned man in the middle of the desert that he can have water,—if he can make the 200 mile journey on foot, alone, to the nearest oasis.

The lies of worthlessness are often buried (or have been stuffed) deep in the heart, making them hard to get to.

Sometimes the pain of rejection is entwined with rage, bitterness, unresolved sin or depression… all of which must be carefully unwound before the strands of worthlessness can be untied. (We've dealt with these issues in the previous chapters.)

So how do we go from being a "head Christian" to one who "loves the lord our God with all our heart, soul, and mind?" (Matthew 22:37). How do we receive that which we hunger for but don't believe we can have?

First, it's important to understand what we're after. From birth, our hearts are "more deceitful than all else and desperately sick" (Jeremiah 17:9) and filled with "evil thoughts, murders, adulteries, fornications, thefts, false witness and slanders" (Matthew 15:19). This sickness of the heart isn't something where we can work two programs, get a little counseling, and feel better in the morning. We're after nothing less than a new heart and there's only one Master Surgeon who can provide it:

Moreover, I will give you a new heart and put a
new spirit within you; and I will remove the heart of stone
from your flesh and give you a heart of flesh.

Ezekiel 36:26

Set your hope on the Master Surgeon. Ask God to reveal what you really believe, expose every lie within, remove them, and then fill your heart with His love. Don't get caught up in focusing on the tools He might use to operate (such as counseling, books, God's Word and other people), look to Him. I suggest that you stop right now and go one-on-one with God; ask Him for the new heart you desire.

As the Lord exposes the root lies, write them out in your journal, and share what He's revealed with your accountability group. Ask them to pray that God would root out the specific lies you've bought into, and replace them with the truth.

Those who know us best can see our blind spots more clearly. Your spouse is the one person in the world who knows you intimately; listen to what they have to say without being defensive. Years ago, Michelle joined me in a session with a counselor. When he asked her why she thought I had a hard time receiving love, without hesitation Michelle said, "Because he doesn't believe he deserves it."

My wife hit the nail on the head; unfortunately, I wasn't in a place where I could hear it. Listen to your spouse. God has given her or him to you for a reason, and they can play a powerful role in the healing process.

Assuming you believe that Jesus died on the cross for your sins, let's look at how God sees YOU. Get alone with God, and ask Him to speak to your heart as you absorb the following. Read carefully and slowly, realizing that the following words are for YOU:

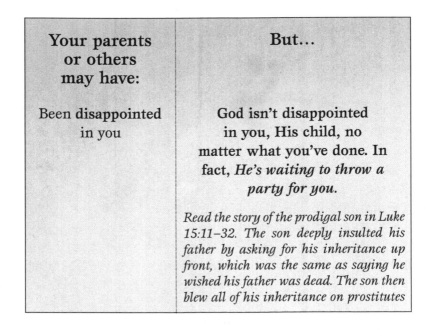

Your parents or others may have:	But...
Been disappointed in you	God isn't disappointed in you, His child, no matter what you've done. In fact, *He's waiting to throw a party for you.*
	Read the story of the prodigal son in Luke 15:11–32. The son deeply insulted his father by asking for his inheritance up front, which was the same as saying he wished his father was dead. The son then blew all of his inheritance on prostitutes

and partying. In spite of this, when his son returned home his father threw a party for him! Although the son had messed up badly, his father loved him deeply; not one word of disappointment or judgment was spoken. No matter where you are today, God is waiting for you to come to Him so He can shower you with an extravagant party of grace.

Been distant

God has always been close to you.

*But as for me,
the nearness of God is my good;
I have made the
Lord God my refuge.*
PSALMS 73:28

You may have been neglected growing up. Perhaps one of your parents died and you've always wondered "where were you God?" You struggle with the idea that God is around... or that you matter enough for Him to be around for you. He has always been near, and He's close to you now. Ask Him to reveal His presence to you.

Been unapproachable

God wants you to come to him.

Let us therefore draw near with confidence to the throne of grace, that we may receive mercy and may find grace to help in time of need.
HEBREWS 4:16

God wants you to come to Him because He loves you and wants to help you. He's not like broken men and women, who get irritated, impatient, and short tempered if we don't have it all together, or mess up. Mercy and comfort await you at the throne of grace; you need not be afraid to approach Him.

Been absent

The Lord will never leave you.

…for He Himself has said,
"I will never desert you,
nor will I ever forsake you."
HEBREWS 13:5

"Am I a God Who is near, declares the Lord, and not a God far off?…
Do I not fill the heaven and the earth?"
JEREMIAH 23:23–24

God is not a workaholic father or mother who is never around. You matter to Him, and He is here for you, now.

Rejected you

God has completely accepted you because of the cross of Christ.

Therefore there is now no condemnation for those who are in Christ Jesus.
ROMANS 8:1

Therefore accept one another just as also Christ accepted us to the glory of God.
ROMANS 15:7

The cross is the most powerful event in history. At the cross Jesus wiped the slate clean and provided abundant entry into heaven for those of us who believe in Him. His acceptance of you is not based on anything but His sacrificial death, and your sin can't erase His acceptance of you. He will not reject you if you approach Him.

Abandoned you

God has taken you up.

*For my father and my mother
have forsaken me,
but the Lord will take me up.*
PSALMS 27:10

*A father of the fatherless
and a judge for the widows,
is God in His holy habitation."*
PSALMS 68:5

*...for He Himself has said
"I will never desert you,
nor will I ever forsake you."*
HEBREWS 13:5

Maybe your parents divorced, and you assumed that "Mom or Dad didn't stick around because of me." Perhaps you were adopted, and suffer with the idea that you were cast aside, unwanted and rejected. Or maybe you were abandoned to the streets at an early age. God will never abandon you, and I believe He's drawing you to Him right now.

Been a **perfectionist**, demanding the same from you for their approval or love.	**God knows you're a mess (Romans 3:23) and can never be perfect, and has showered you with the free gift of His grace.** *For by grace you have been saved through faith, and that not of yourselves it is the gift of God.* EPHESIANS 2:8 *and hope does not disappoint, because the love of God has been poured out within our hearts through the Holy Spirit who was given to us."* ROMANS 5:5 *God knows you've sinned and will never be perfect. He doesn't point fingers, reject, bash you with Bible verses, or demand perfection, like other broken, imperfect men and women have done. You can stop trying to measure up to an impossible standard and accept the big, brightly wrapped gift of grace God has for YOU.*
Abused you	**God wants to comfort you, if you let Him.** *I, even I am He Who comforts you.* ISAIAH 51:12 *He comforts the traumatized, the abused, and the neglected. You won't get hurt if you approach Him; He's not out to use you. He will comfort you, if you will take a chance and drop your guard.*

Failed to love to you in word or deed.	God loves YOU passionately.
	But God who is rich in mercy, because of His great love with which He loved us, even when we were dead in trespasses made us alive together in Christ. EPHESIANS 2:4–5
	Just as the Father has loved Me, I have also loved you; abide in My love. JOHN 15:9
	This is My commandment, that you love one another, just as I have loved you. JOHN 15:12
	But I would feed you with the finest of the wheat and with honey from the rock I would satisfy you. PSALMS 81:16
	For God so loved the world, that He gave His only begotten Son, that whoever believes in Him shall not perish, but have eternal life. JOHN 3:16
	Because Thy lovingkindness is better than life. PSALMS 63:3

Anyone who would send His Son to be butchered for another person either hates his Son, or passionately loves the one who He sent his Son to die for. Since we know that the Father loves His Son, Jesus Christ, the only possible answer is that God loves you deeply.

The problem has been that you've bought into the lies that God's love is conditional, or impossible for you to attain, or that you'll get hurt if you're vulnerable, or that you sinned too much for God to love you. None of this lines up with God's word.

You may be imprisoned in shame because of a sexual crime; maybe you've raped, molested, or killed someone. The cross is infinitely bigger than your sin, and God accepts you. Or maybe you've committed adultery and lost your family. The blood of Christ has wiped out your debt, and there's a party waiting to be held in your honor.

Forget about how you feel and the lies you've bought into; look at the truth. The door to your prison of shame and worthlessness has been swung wide open, and you need only to walk out into the light. There's no hoop to jump through, no test to pass; just the acceptance of a gift. You have to decide if you will accept the truth that He loves you passionately, or if you'll remain in the prison of shame and condemnation.

Perhaps you're broken by the realization that you've been saying, "I don't believe you love me God; it can't be true." Speak to Abba now and confess that you've been turning Him away; allow Him to comfort you. Mercy and love await you at the throne of grace.

If you're still struggling with accepting God's love, don't worry. The Father doesn't stop waiting for you to come home "because you didn't get it right the first time." The sanctification process isn't often a one-time slam dunk event; a little more time may be needed for Him to dig deeper and loosen the roots. Or there could be something you're still holding onto that is keeping you from accepting the gift of grace (we'll touch on this in chapter 13). Keep seeking The Master Surgeon, and don't give up; He's got a party waiting for you....

chapter eleven

God
of Grace

~

GRACE: A FAVOR RENDERED BY ONE WHO NEED NOT DO SO;
INDULGENCE... DIVINE LOVE AND PROTECTION BESTOWED FREELY
ON PEOPLE... THE STATE OF BEING PROTECTED OR SANCTIFIED BY
THE FAVOR OF GOD...AN EXCELLENCE OR POWER GRANTED BY GOD.

The American Heritage® Dictionary of the English Language,
Fourth Edition

In Matthew 25, Jesus tells us the parable of the talents. A Greek talent was a measurement of money by weight, estimated to be 75 pounds. Before leaving on a long journey, a master gives three of his slaves a portion of his money to trade with, in hope they will make a return for him. One slave is given five talents of money, the second, two talents, and the third slave is given one talent.

We don't know if the master doled his talents out in gold or silver, but either way, it was a hefty sum. A talent of silver in today's money would be worth $42,000.00, while a talent of gold would tip the scales at $1,800,000.00.[1] The master was entrusting his slaves with a lot of his treasure.

The first two slaves immediately went out and doubled their master's money. Upon his return, the master heaped the same words of praise and reward on both men: "Well done, good and faithful slave. You were faithful with a few things, I will put you in charge of many things; enter into the joy of your master" (Matthew 25:21).

However, the slave who had been given one talent took his master's money, dug a hole in the ground, and buried all 56 pounds of it there. This would have been no small task, being he first had to haul the heavy load of coins to a secret burial place, and then dig a hole wide and deep enough to "store it."

The results of this slave's "stewardship" were disastrous:

And the one also who had received the one talent came up and said, "Master, I knew you to be a hard man, reaping where you did not sow and gathering where you scattered no seed. And I was afraid, and went away and hid your talent in the ground. See, you have what is yours." But his master answered and said to him, "You wicked, lazy slave, you knew that I reap where I did not sow and gather where I scattered no seed. Then you ought to have put my money in the bank, and on my arrival I would have received my money back with interest. Therefore take away the talent from him, and give it to the one who has the ten talents. For to everyone who has, more shall be given, and he will have an abundance; but from the one who does not have, even what he does have shall be taken away. Throw out the worthless slave into the outer darkness; in that place there will be weeping and gnashing of teeth.

MATTHEW 25:24–30

In the end, the third slave's one-sided, distorted view of His master's character caused him to be cast into a place of darkness and "weeping and gnashing of teeth." From his attitude of fear and resentment, one must question if he really knew his master at all.

For the first 36 years of my life, my view of God was little different than the third slave's. I knew the Lord was holy and hated sin, but I had a miserable time seeing Him as a God of grace and love. I saw Him as a "hard man" who closely watched me for every mistake. When I would fall into sexual sin, I would often cower in fear, waiting for the hammer of judgment to drop. After all, didn't God flatten Sodom and Gomorrah because of sexual depravity and wickedness?

Sodom was judged, but God's wrath is just one side of His multi-faceted character. If we don't see the Lord as He truly is, we are no better than the third slave; we'll struggle with accepting God's forgiveness and grace, and our hearts will harden in resentment toward Him. We'll be in danger of becoming a "wicked, lazy slave" who would rather bury 56 pounds of gold in the dirt than earn a return on it.

Is the Lord a God of grace, or is He a "hard man?" There are a number of stories in the Bible that reveal the character traits of God as surely as they show us the humanness of the key players.

Adam and Eve

When God made Adam and Eve, He could have said "let's see how long you'll last" and set them in a place like Death Valley, California, where the temperatures can reach 120 degrees in summer, or Siberia, which can go as low as 70 below zero in winter. Instead, He provided them with a tropical paradise for their home. In Genesis 2:8–10 we read:

The Lord God planted a garden toward the east, in Eden; and there He placed the man whom He had formed. Out of the ground the Lord God caused to grow every tree that is pleasing to the sight and good for food; the tree of life also

*in the midst of the garden, and the tree of the knowledge of
good and evil. Now a river flowed out of Eden to water the
garden; and from there it divided and became four rivers.*

I've seen beautiful man-made gardens that knocked my
socks off; one created by God must have been breathtaking.
Adam and Eve had "every tree that is pleasing to the sight
and good for food." There would have been exquisite flowers
set in lush green foliage, majestic trees filled with colorful
birds, delicious exotic fruit trees, and hearty vegetable plants.
The sound of rushing water from the river that originated
from Eden would have been heard in much of the garden,
along with the chorus of birds and other animals. It would
have been a joyful existence, like living in Maui or Tahiti
without all the high costs.

Adam and Eve also had the incredible blessing of enjoying
God's presence on a consistent basis. In Genesis 3:8 we read
"they heard the sound of the Lord God walking in the garden
in the cool of the day." (Sadly, this was after they'd blown it.)
Evidently, they took walks together with the Lord in the late
afternoons; He enjoyed spending time with His creation.

From the start, God showered Adam and Eve with blessings. There was no sickness, sorrow, pain, fear, or death
before the fall; all of their needs were provided for in abundant splendor. God's actions revealed a desire to bless His
creation with the best life has to offer—which included the
joy of His Presence.

Then, Adam and Eve sinned by eating fruit from the one tree
God had told them not to. After lavishing them with His best
and watching them fall, God could have said, "Well, Adam and
Eve 1.0 didn't work, let's delete these two and run version 2.0."

But He didn't. Although Adam and Eve reaped the consequences for their actions, God continued to "freely bestow
His divine love and protection" on them. His first act was to

provide them with clothing, which He did by killing an animal. God's grace, His "favor rendered by one who need not do so" didn't stop after they had sinned.

Cain

Adam and Eve's first born son was named Cain; later they had Abel, their second son. While they most probably had other sons and daughters, the Bible story focuses on the maturing of these two boys.

So it came about in the course of time that Cain brought an offering to the Lord of the fruit of the ground. Abel, on his part also brought of the firstlings of his flock and of their fat portions. And the Lord had regard for Abel and for his offering; but for Cain and for his offering He had no regard. So Cain became very angry and his countenance fell. Then the Lord said to Cain, "Why are you angry? And why has your countenance fallen? If you do well, will not your countenance be lifted up? And if you do not do well, sin is crouching at the door; and its desire is for you, but you must master it."

Genesis 4:3–7

Cain had problems with pride and anger; he wanted to do things his way and he didn't listen to God's instruction or warnings—even when doing things his way blew up in his face. Unfortunately Cain's pride-induced blindness set his life on a course to tragic ruin, as he later murdered his brother. Strike one.

Knowing the consequences his parents faced after their original sin, you'd think Cain would have been fearful of what God might do next. Yet, when the Lord approached Cain after he'd killed Abel and said, "Where is Abel your brother?" Cain replied "I do not know. Am I my brother's keeper?" (Genesis 4:9). Cain was saying, "Up yours, who cares?"—strikes two and three in one breath.

If I were God, Cain's out; there's no way I'm letting this bozo get away with blowing me off, especially after I'd warned him. It's fire and brimstone time; Cain's going to be darker and crispier than a marshmallow that's been roasted with a flamethrower. And, if I were God I'm surely not going to record what Cain said in my book for everyone to see; it might make my reputation look weak.

But God's response was nothing like what I would have done.

> He (God) said, "What have you done? The voice of your brother's blood is crying to Me from the ground.
> "Now you are cursed from the ground, which has opened its mouth to receive your brother's blood from your hand.
> "When you cultivate the ground, it will no longer yield its strength to you; you will be a vagrant and a wanderer on the earth." Cain said to the Lord, "My punishment is too great to bear! Behold, You have driven me this day from the face of the ground; and from Your face I will be hidden, and I will be a vagrant and a wanderer on the earth, and whoever finds me will kill me." So the Lord said to him, "Therefore whoever kills Cain, vengeance will be taken on him sevenfold." And the Lord appointed a sign for Cain, so that no one finding him would slay him. Then Cain went out from the presence of the Lord, and settled in the land of Nod, east of Eden. Cain had relations with his wife and she conceived, and gave birth to Enoch; and he built a city, and called the name of the city Enoch, after the name of his son.

GENESIS 4:10–17

Cain suffered serious consequences for his sin; it appears he never saw his parents again, and he lost his ability to grow food. Yet, the Lord provided Cain with protection from anyone who might try to kill him and blessed his future. Cain had a wife, raised a family and built a city. Cain deserved death, yet he received "protection and sanctification by the favor of God."

Sodom and Gomorrah

I can hear it now. You're saying, "Wait a minute, God wasted Sodom and Gomorrah; what does grace have to do with them?!"

In Genesis 18 we read the story of where God revealed his intention with Sodom and Gomorrah to Abraham. Lot, Abraham's nephew, was living in Sodom, and Abraham was desperate to see Lot's life preserved:

Abraham came near and said, "Will You indeed sweep away the righteous with the wicked?" Suppose there are fifty righteous within the city; will You indeed sweep it away and not spare the place for the sake of the fifty righteous who are in it? "Far be it from You to do such a thing, to slay the righteous with the wicked, so that the righteous and the wicked are treated alike. Far be it from You! Shall not the Judge of all the earth deal justly?" So the Lord said, "If I find in Sodom fifty righteous within the city, then I will spare the whole place on their account." And Abraham replied, "Now behold, I have ventured to speak to the Lord, although I am but dust and ashes. "Suppose the fifty righteous are lacking five, will You destroy the whole city because of five?" And He said, "I will not destroy it if I find forty-five there." He spoke to Him yet again and said, "Suppose forty are found there?" And He said, "I will not do it on account of the forty." Then he said, "Oh may the Lord not be angry, and I shall speak; suppose thirty are found there?" And He said, "I will not do it if I find thirty there." And he said, "Now behold, I have ventured to speak to the Lord; suppose twenty are found there?" And He said, "I will not destroy it on account of the twenty." Then he said, "Oh may the Lord not be angry, and I shall speak only this

once; suppose ten are found there?" And He said,
"I will not destroy it on account of the ten."

GENESIS 18:23–32

God wasn't jumping at the prospect of destroying Sodom; He was willing to spare the city for 10 righteous persons. In the end, not even 10 persons could be found, and Lot escaped with his two daughters.

In Ezekiel 33:11, God reveals His heart in relation to judgment:

"Say to them, 'As I live!' declares the Lord God,
'I take no pleasure in the death of the wicked, but rather
that the wicked turn from his way and live. Turn back,
turn back from your evil ways!'"

The people of Sodom were so thoroughly saturated with perversion and wickedness that there was no hope the light of God's love could penetrate their hearts; to allow the city to remain would be to risk that others might be taken down the same path of sin and destruction. Sodom corrupted all who entered the city, including Lot's family, as his daughters showed by their actions after they fled the city.

Lot went up from Zoar, and stayed in the mountains, and his
two daughters with him; for he was afraid to stay in Zoar; and
he stayed in a cave, he and his two daughters. Then the
firstborn said to the younger, "Our father is old, and there is
not a man on earth to come in to us after the manner of the
earth. "Come, let us make our father drink wine, and let us lie
with him that we may preserve our family through our father."
So they made their father drink wine that night, and the
firstborn went in and lay with her father; and he did not know
when she lay down or when she arose. On the following day,
the firstborn said to the younger, "Behold, I lay last night with

my father; let us make him drink wine tonight also; then you go in and lie with him, that we may preserve our family through our father." So they made their father drink wine that night also, and the younger arose and lay with him; and he did not know when she lay down or when she arose. Thus both the daughters of Lot were with child by their father.

GENESIS 19:30–36

If Lot and his family had lived in another city with a strong community of believers, his daughters would have been more likely to trust the Lord to extend their father's lineage, rather than resort to incest. Yet, when I look at what happened to Sodom, I see God's grace on display in several ways:

1. He allowed Abraham to petition Him to spare the city.
2. He revealed His grace in that He was willing to spare Sodom for only 10 persons.
3. He showed grace to Lot's *entire* family by sparing them; tragically, only four accepted God's offer to leave the city. As Lot, his wife, and their two daughters were leaving Sodom, one of the angels said, "Escape for your life! Do not look behind you, and do not stay anywhere in the valley; escape to the mountains, or you will be swept away" (Genesis 19:17). Lot's wife disobeyed by looking back at the city of sin, and was turned into a pillar of salt.
4. The destruction of Sodom protected others from being corrupted.
5. When Lot's daughters sinned by having sex with their father, God showed grace to their children by making them the fathers of two new nations, both of which would later become enemies of the Nation of Israel (Moab and Ammon). In spite of this, the Lord would later honor a woman from the nation of Moab, Ruth, by

devoting an entire book of the Bible to her story; she was also honored in the bloodline of Jesus (Matthew 1:5).

Though we don't read it in Scriptures, I wouldn't be surprised if the Lord wept when Sodom was destroyed.

Rahab

As Joshua 2:1 reveals, Rahab was a prostitute in Jericho, another city destined for judgment:

Then Joshua the son of Nun sent two men as spies secretly from Shittim, saying, "Go, view the land, especially Jericho." So they went and came into the house of a harlot whose name was Rahab, and lodged there.

According to the law God provided the nation of Israel in Leviticus 20, Rahab deserved the death penalty for her sexual sin. What could a prostitute do to become a recipient of God's grace?

It was told the king of Jericho, saying, "Behold, men from the sons of Israel have come here tonight to search out the land." And the king of Jericho sent word to Rahab, saying, "Bring out the men who have come to you, who have entered your house, for they have come to search out all the land." But the woman had taken the two men and hidden them, and she said, "Yes, the men came to me, but I did not know where they were from. "It came about when {it was time} to shut the gate at dark, that the men went out; I do not know where the men went. Pursue them quickly, for you will overtake them." But she had brought them up to the roof and hidden them in the stalks of flax which she had laid in order on the roof. So the men pursued them on the road to the Jordan to the fords; and as soon as those who were pursuing them had gone out, they shut the gate.

Now before they lay down, she came up to them on the roof and said to the men, "I know that the Lord has given you the land,

and that the terror of you has fallen on us, and that all the
inhabitants of the land have melted away before you. " For we
have heard how the Lord dried up the water of the Red Sea
before you when you came out of Egypt, and what you did to
the two kings of the Amorites who were beyond the Jordan, to
Sihon and Og, whom you utterly destroyed. When we heard it,
our hearts melted and no courage remained in any man
any longer because of you; for the Lord your God,
He is God in heaven above and on earth beneath.

JOSHUA 2:2–11

At first glance it might seem that Rahab earned God's grace by hiding the spies, but there's more to it than this. Before the spies stumbled onto her abode, Rahab had believed that "He is God in heaven above and on earth beneath" from hearing of the Lord's mighty work for Israel. More than a thousand years later, the writer of Hebrews clarifies that it was Rahab's faith that saved her:

By faith Rahab the harlot did not perish along with those who
were disobedient, after she had welcomed the spies in peace.

HEBREWS 11:31

It was "by faith" that Rahab survived, not from hiding the spies; her act of kindness was the outflow of her belief in the Living God of grace, not the reverse. Rahab was the only one who came to a saving knowledge of God out of the entire population of Jericho, even though they all heard the same news about God's work. The difference was that they hardened their hearts.

And without faith it is impossible to please Him,
for he who comes to God must believe that He is
and that He is a rewarder of those who seek Him.

HEBREWS 11:6

A man or woman with a hard heart will not see the Lord as a God of grace who "rewards those who seek Him"; they'll react in anger, as Cain did, or fear like the people of Jericho. A man with a hard heart is unwilling to repent, and unwillingness to repent is blatant rebellion and disobedience against God. As Hebrews 11:31 describes, it is the disobedient who perish.

Rahab, by the way, was still a prostitute when the spies approached her; she hadn't yet cleaned up her life. Read Joshua 2:1 again:

> *So they went and came into the house of a harlot*
> *whose name was Rahab, and lodged there.*

The text doesn't say, "they came into the house of a former harlot named Rahab…" which means she was still practicing her trade. God honored Rahab's newborn, mustard seed-sized faith that He was a "rewarder of those who seek Him" with His "divine love and protection." Rahab walked away from sexual sin after she'd received the gift of grace.

We know Rahab left her life of prostitution because she later married a Jew named Salmon; he wouldn't have married her if she were still a prostitute. Salmon, by the way, was the great-grandfather of David, who was in Jesus' earthly father's bloodline (Matthew 1:1–6).

There are five women in the entire genealogy of Matthew 1: Tamar, who posed as a prostitute to have sex with her father-in-law, Rahab, the former prostitute, Ruth of Moab, a nation founded on incest, Bathsheba, the married woman who committed adultery with David, and Mary—who was judged for being an unwed mother (John 8:41). Perhaps God intentionally placed so many of the sexually broken in Jesus' human ancestry because He wanted to show us that, like them, we too can be recipients of His "divine love and protec-tion… bestowed freely on people."

154

Manasseh

Manasseh was raised by Hezekiah, king of Judah, a righteous man who loved God. In spite of his upbringing, Manasseh threw himself into satanic worship and debauchery, as we read in 2 Chronicles 33:1–7:

Manasseh was twelve years old when he became king, and he reigned fifty-five years in Jerusalem. He did evil in the sight of the Lord according to the abominations of the nations whom the Lord dispossessed before the sons of Israel. For he rebuilt the high places which Hezekiah his father had broken down; he also erected altars for the Baals and made Asherim, and worshiped all the host of heaven and served them. He built altars in the house of the Lord of which the Lord had said, "My name shall be in Jerusalem forever." For he built altars for all the host of heaven in the two courts of the house of the Lord. He made his sons pass through the fire in the valley of Ben-hinnom; and he practiced witchcraft, used divination, practiced sorcery and dealt with mediums and spiritists. He did much evil in the sight of the Lord, provoking Him to anger. Then he put the carved image of the idol which he had made in the house of God…

Manasseh was a male witch who burned his own children to death, killed many innocent people and put up demonic idols throughout the nation of Israel—one he placed in the temple of God. Manasseh participated in satanic, sexual rites with temple prostitutes. This guy threw his sin in God's face with complete abandon, and with predictable results. Manasseh "provoked the Lord to anger" more than the heathen nations who didn't know God (2 Kings 21:11).

I don't know about you, but the thought of getting the Creator of the Universe angry with me isn't a pleasant thought. If anyone deserved to be fire and brim-stoned, it was Manasseh.

2 Chronicles 33:11–16 reveals what God did, and how Manasseh responded:

Therefore the Lord brought the commanders of the army of the king of Assyria against them, and they captured Manasseh with hooks, bound him with bronze chains and took him to Babylon. When he was in distress, he entreated the Lord his God and humbled himself greatly before the God of his fathers. When he prayed to Him, He was moved by his entreaty and heard his supplication, and brought him again to Jerusalem to his kingdom. Then Manasseh knew that the Lord was God. Now after this he built the outer wall of the city of David on the west side of Gihon, in the valley, even to the entrance of the Fish Gate; and he encircled the Ophel with it and made it very high. Then he put army commanders in all the fortified cities of Judah. He also removed the foreign gods and the idol from the house of the Lord, as well as all the altars which he had built on the mountain of the house of the Lord and in Jerusalem, and he threw them outside the city. He set up the altar of the Lord and sacrificed peace offerings and thank offerings on it; and he ordered Judah to serve the Lord God of Israel.

Now why in the world would God give someone like Manasseh a second chance? He surely didn't deserve it, but then, grace—"a favor rendered by one who need not do so"— has nothing to do with earning love. Manasseh took on heavy consequences for his sin, yet when he "entreated the Lord his God and humbled himself greatly before the God of his fathers," God brought Manasseh home and used him powerfully. Revitalized by grace, this former warlock/baby killer/murderer/hedonist/ rebuilt the nation and led them in spiritual revival!

Like Rahab, Manasseh is also shown in Jesus' earthly bloodline in Matthew 1:10; another sinner redeemed by "the excellence and power granted by God."

Peter

Peter had it made. Jesus had promised him "the keys to the kingdom of heaven" (Matthew 16:19), and that he would judge the 12 tribes of Israel (Matthew 19:28). Problem was, Peter's head got big, and pride (as we know from Proverbs 16:18) is a set up for a big fall. When Peter hit the pavement, everyone was watching.

While Jesus was being tried by the Jewish Sanhedrin in a public place, Peter was asked three times by three different persons if he knew Jesus. Peter responded to each situation by denying that he knew the Lord—the last time with swearing. In Matthew 10:33, Jesus had said: "But whoever denies Me before men, I will also deny him before My Father who is in heaven." Peter must have been pierced by these words, humiliated from denying Jesus in public, and ashamed by his bold promise at the last supper that he would die with Jesus rather than deny him. What must have cut Peter the deepest was looking Jesus in the eye after denying Him the third time, as the last curse words left his lips:

After about an hour had passed, another man began to insist, saying, "Certainly this man also was with Him, for he is a Galilean too." But Peter said, "Man, I do not know what you are talking about." Immediately, while he was still speaking, a rooster crowed. The Lord turned and looked at Peter. And Peter remembered the word of the Lord, how He had told him, "Before a rooster crows today, you will deny Me three times." And he went out and wept bitterly.

LUKE 22:59–62

Condemned by his own words and filled with shame, Peter would have been terrified of what Jesus might do.

Jesus' response was amazing. There was no lecture, no finger pointing, no "I told you so and why didn't you listen when I warned you?" Instead, Jesus met Peter where he was—dirty, broken and writhing in shame—and asked but one question three times: "do you love me?" (John 21). I marvel at how Jesus gently restored Peter with such tender love, even as He cut into the pride and people-pleasing deep in Peter's heart. Jesus was saying, "Do you love Me more than other people? Do you love Me more than your want for personal glory? Will you make Me the biggest thing in your life, no matter what the cost or what others say?" Peter was challenged to make Jesus his first love, and he did so. As a result, God used Peter in many powerful ways, which are recorded in the book of Acts.

Later, when he penned the books of first and second Peter through the influence of the Holy Spirit, Peter wrote:

And all of you, clothe yourselves with humility toward one another, for God is opposed to the proud, but gives grace to the humble. Therefore humble yourselves under the mighty hand of God, that he may exalt you at the proper time, casting all your anxiety on him, because he cares for you.

1 PETER 5:5–7

Now that we've accumulated the evidence of the Lord's track record with broken men and women, let's assemble the case so we can see Him as He is.

1. God gives us His best.

We saw the Lord's desire to give us His best when He set Adam and Eve down in paradise, and we see it today in His majestic mountains, glowing sunsets, forests of green, roaring seas, and tranquil deserts. He provided us with all the nutrients our bodies need for a long, healthy life from a variety of sources (plants, trees, and wildlife). He gave us powerful minds that can learn, discover, and engineer the things that make life easier, as well as the resources to build them with. He created woman "because it's not good for man to be alone"; sex for pleasure in marriage, and the joy of children. Music, and those who are blessed with the ability to create it, is another gift of His best. His Word is His best; He spent some 1,400 years putting it together so that we who live today could know Him. The list of His best for us is endless.

After we sinned and rebelled against Him, God gave us the best of His best—the sacrifice of His Son, through which we can have life to the fullest and one day enjoy the everlasting pleasure of being with Him in Heaven.

2. His grace outshines our most wretched sin.

The favor shown to Manasseh amazes me. The Lord extended grace to a man who spitefully rebelled against Him in every way possible by worshipping Satan, murdering children and adults, reveling in sexual sin, placing demonic images in the temple—and leading God's chosen people to do the same. Such grace for someone so evil and depraved is almost too incredible for me to comprehend—which is the point. God's grace is bigger, wider, and deeper than we can understand—more wonderful than we can hope for.

3. His love cannot be earned or deserved.

You will not find anything Adam and Eve, Cain, Lot, Rahab, Manasseh, Peter or anyone else in Scripture did to earn or deserve God's grace. None of them tried to earn it, buy it, or deserve it, and neither should we.

4. Our sin doesn't stop God from loving us.

The Lord was kind to Cain, even as he angrily lied to His face about killing Abel (think about that one). The men of Sodom were committing sexual sin as Abraham asked for the city to be spared. And Jesus looked at Peter, right after he denied the Lord with cursing. How many of us love like that?

5. God's grace doesn't nullify His holiness
or remove the consequences of sin.

After they fell and were banished from the Garden of Eden, Adam and Eve infected the entire human race with sin; the damage from their decision to disobey God was severe, extensive and irrevocable. Cain "went out from the presence of the Lord," may not have seen his parents again, and was unable to harvest food from the ground. Rahab and Manasseh would have had to deal with the physical, emotional and mental scarring (not to mention the public stigma) from their life of sin. After denying Christ three times, Peter's reputation would have been ruined; in spite of how God used him afterwards, Peter is often remembered the most by his failure.

We reap what we sow (Galatians 6:7); if we thrust our hand in the flames of sin, it will get burned.

6. The Lord patiently meets us where we are,
even if we're in a mud hole.

The Lord approached Adam and Eve while they were hiding in shame, then put up with their attempts to deflect the responsibility from their sin. I wouldn't have been as patient while they played the blame game, as my kids might testify. Rahab was still a prostitute when the two spies showed up at her door; if I were God, I might have been tempted to wait before she turned off the red light in her home before freely bestowing my "divine protection" on her. Jesus restored Peter when he must have been withering in shame, fear and doubt—without waiting for an apology or confession of sin.

If cleaning up our lives were a requirement to receive God's grace, we'd all be in serious trouble.

7. God gently restores the broken.

I have always marveled at how kind Jesus was when He restored Peter. The Lord's love is amazing in that someone He loved could deny Him so vehemently and yet He restored Peter without a trace of resentment or bitterness.

If I heard my wife say, "I don't know Mike" or "I don't love him" three times to another person (especially to another man), I would be insane with hurt and anger. Jesus must have been deeply grieved when Peter denied Him.

What amazing love, what compassion He has for those of us who praise Him one moment, then deny him the next with porn or lust. Truly, the Lord's "kindness leads us to repentance" (Romans 2:4).

8. God showers His love on the sexually broken.

From the men and women listed in Jesus' bloodline, doesn't it seem as though He made a special effort to expose His desire to give grace to the sexually broken? Throughout Scripture, the Lord showed that prostitutes, adulterers, and sex offenders (which is what Manasseh would have been) are all welcome to dine at the table of His divine love and favor. Perhaps the Lord included so many stories of the sexually broken because He wants to break through the cloud of shame and rejection they live under with the light of His love.

9. God seeks those who are lost.

The Lord sought Adam and Eve—as they were hiding in shame. He approached Abraham and told him of the coming judgment on Sodom, and later sent two angels to Sodom to extract Lot and his family from the city before it was destroyed. God sought Rahab by revealing the truth of who He is to her, and then guiding the two spies to her home. God pulled Manasseh, a man who "provoked Him to anger more than the heathen nations" to Him with hooks and chains, rather than allow him to be killed in battle. And after making breakfast for the apostles on the beach, Jesus gently restored Peter.

Today, I know that the Lord was seeking me even as I was running the other way. If you examine the circumstances of your life, I'll bet you'll see that He's been after you too.

For the Son of Man has come to seek
and to save that which was lost.

LUKE 19:10

10. We have a choice as to how we will see God.

God's undeserved favor towards man is everywhere; in the splendor of His provision for us, in His kindness towards others who've sinned throughout history, and in the gift of His Son on the cross. In spite of this, there are many who, like the third slave, still choose to see the Lord as a "hard man." God doesn't force anyone to see Him as He is—we are given the freedom to choose whether we will view Him as a God of grace, or buy into Satan's lies.

Those who harden their hearts against His love are in danger of being recipients of His wrath, because to see Him as a "hard man" is to spitefully reject Him, and His love for us.

By the way, in the parable of the talents we don't read where the master took his original money or the profits back from the first two slaves. They apparently kept it all, in addition to receiving more blessings. Their master showed no interest in taking it back; He was undoubtedly rich, having initially given his three slaves 448 pounds of gold or silver coins to invest with. He was not after money, but the true state of each man's heart; to know if they loved Him or not. What they did with His treasure exposed the truth.

11. We can approach Him, no matter what we've done or how ashamed we feel.

When Jesus appeared to Peter on the beach, Peter, who was fishing in a boat one hundred yards away, "threw himself into the sea" and swam for Jesus. It was on the beach, face to face with Jesus, where Peter's life was changed.

In the next chapter, we shall do the same, and draw near to the Lord.

chapter twelve

Come to Me

❧

"WHERE SIN AND SORROW STOPS, AND THE SONG OF THE SAINT
STARTS. DO I REALLY WANT TO GET THERE? I CAN RIGHT NOW.
THE QUESTIONS THAT TRULY MATTER IN LIFE ARE REMARKABLY
FEW, AND THEY ARE ALL ANSWERED BY THESE WORDS—"COME
TO ME." OUR LORD'S WORDS ARE NOT, "DO THIS, OR DON'T DO
THAT," BUT—"COME TO ME." IF I WILL SIMPLY COME TO JESUS,
MY REAL LIFE WILL BE BROUGHT INTO HARMONY WITH MY
REAL DESIRES. I WILL ACTUALLY CEASE FROM SIN, AND WILL
FIND THE SONG OF THE LORD BEGINNING IN MY LIFE.

HAVE YOU EVER COME TO JESUS? LOOK AT THE STUBBORNNESS OF
YOUR HEART. YOU WOULD RATHER DO ANYTHING THAN THIS ONE
SIMPLE CHILDLIKE THING—"COME TO ME." IF YOU REALLY WANT TO
EXPERIENCE CEASING FROM SIN, YOU MUST COME TO JESUS.

JESUS CHRIST MAKES HIMSELF THE TEST TO DETERMINE YOUR GEN-
UINENESS. LOOK AT HOW HE USES THE WORD COME. AT THE MOST
UNEXPECTED MOMENTS IN YOUR LIFE THERE IS THIS WHISPER OF
THE LORD—"COME TO ME," AND YOU ARE IMMEDIATELY DRAWN TO
HIM. PERSONAL CONTACT WITH JESUS CHANGES EVERYTHING. BE
'FOOLISH' ENOUGH TO COME AND COMMIT YOURSELF TO WHAT HE
SAYS. THE ATTITUDE NECESSARY FOR YOU TO COME TO HIM IS ONE
WHERE YOUR WILL HAS MADE THE DETERMINATION TO LET GO OF
EVERYTHING AND DELIBERATELY COMMIT IT ALL TO HIM."[1]

Oswald Chambers, from My Utmost for His Highest.

It was June, 1999. Since January I'd gone all out in the battle against lust; my life was packed with accountability with other men, and I'd dealt with a traumatic father wound issue. It had been nearly six months since my last porn binge, yet in spite of all this I was still empty. Although the poison within was gone, the pull to lust remained, lurking beneath the surface.

I'd gone on a manic search for a way to fill the void inside by doing ministry work. I went on a short-term missions trip to China, and then served at the local rescue mission as a volunteer. Still empty.

Confused, I sought Brian's advice.

"I've been doing all these things but am still empty; it feels like I'm looking for God," I said.

Brian smiled… "You won't find Him there."

The light went on; I'd been trying to find God by doing things for Him. My "know the Bible and be good enough" version of Christianity had left me starved for something far more transcendent, powerful, and life changing. I was hungry for God, and knowing about Him was no longer enough. For the first time in my life, I launched in a full bore, no-holds-barred search for God. I didn't have a clear understanding of what searching for God looked like, but at least I'd dismounted the treadmill of "doing to be loved."

I started by searching for clues in His Word as to how I could find Him, and He provided them in abundance. As I tore through the Psalms, the verses about seeking God were like runway lights to a pilot on a dark night:

The Lord has looked down from heaven upon the sons of men to see if there are any who understand, who seek after God.
PSALMS 14:2

When You said, "Seek My face," my heart said to You,
"Your face, O Lord, I shall seek."

PSALMS 27:8

O God, You are my God; I shall seek You earnestly;
My soul thirsts for You, my flesh yearns for You,
In a dry and weary land where there is no water.

PSALMS 63:1

How blessed are those who observe His testimonies,
who seek Him with all their heart. They also do
no unrighteousness; they walk in His ways.

PSALMS 119:2–3

I went outside the Psalms and found more verses about seeking the Lord:

But from there you will seek the Lord your God,
and you will find Him if you search for Him
with all your heart and all your soul.

DEUTERONOMY 4:29

You will seek Me and find Me when you search
for Me with all your heart.

JEREMIAH 29:13

Sow with a view to righteousness, reap in accordance with
kindness; break up your fallow ground, For it is time
to seek the Lord Until He comes to rain righteousness on you.

HOSEA 10:12

But seek first His kingdom and His righteousness,
and all these things will be added to you.

MATTHEW 6:33

Ask, and it will be given to you; seek, and you will find; knock,
and it will be opened to you. For everyone who asks receives,

and he who seeks finds, and to him who
knocks it will be opened.

MATTHEW 7:7–8

God had packed His Word from Old Testament to New with invitations to seek Him "with all of the heart," and big promises were attached. Those who sought Him would "do no unrighteousness" and "understand all things"; and He would "rain righteousness" on them. Jesus promised "the other things would be added to them," and that "everyone who asks would receive, those who seek would find, and to him who knocks it would be opened." Most important to me at the time, God promised that I would find Him if I went after Him "with all of my heart."

The "all of my heart" part was convicting. I'd gone after sex, work, money, and other things with zeal before, but had never thought of going after God that way. The years I'd sought freedom from sexual sin I'd completely missed the Lord; I'd wanted Him to free me, but the idea of wanting *Him* never crossed my mind. "All of my heart" exposed that my true affections were for things, people, and feeling good, rather than Him. I felt shallow, like I'd been trying to use God as a gumball machine.

I continued my search in the gospels, focusing on what Jesus said and did. He made spending time with the Father a priority, even if He'd had a full day of ministry (Matthew 14:23, Luke 6:12, 21:37), and He told us that the greatest commandment was to "love the Lord your God with all your heart." I couldn't see Jesus giving up a night of sleep just because He wanted to look good in Scripture, so He must have enjoyed being with the Father.

I drew a blank when it came to enjoying God. How do you enjoy a relationship with someone you can't see? Yet, Jesus did, and He commanded us to do the same. "Love God with all your heart" exposed something missing in my relationship with Him. I'd read the Bible and gone to church, but I was empty; there was no "love for God" like this in my heart.

The more I read the more desperate I became to know Him. I set all of my agendas and lists aside—including my lifelong request for freedom from sexual sin—and went after the Lord, determined not to stop seeking until I found Him. "I want you Lord, please reveal Yourself to me. Please fill me with You. I want to know You; I'm starved for You. I've had enough of my ways, I'm ready for Yours, no matter what... I want You, God!!!"

I sought God all out, asking Him to reveal Himself to me. Some mornings I'd listen to worship music and silently praise Him, other times I'd eat through His Word like a starved man in the wilderness. One morning as I read through the book of First John, the words about God's love stood out like never before:

*Beloved, let us love one another, **for love is from God;** and **everyone who loves is born of God and knows God.** **The one who does not love does not know God, for God is** love. By this **the love of God was manifested in us,** that God has sent His only begotten Son into the world so that we might live through Him. In this is love, not that we loved God, but that **He loved us** and sent His Son to be the propitiation for our sins. Beloved, if God so loved us, we also ought to love one another. No one has seen God at any time; **if we love one** **another, God abides in us, and His love is perfected in us.** By this we know that we abide in Him and He in us, because He has given us of His Spirit. We have seen and testify that the Father has sent the Son to be the Savior of the world. Whoever confesses that Jesus is the Son of God, God abides in him, and he in God. **We have come to know and have believed the love** **which God has for us. God is love, and the one who abides in***

*love abides in God, and God abides in him. By this, love is
perfected with us, so that we may have confidence in the day of
judgment; because as He is, so also are we in this world.
There is no fear in love; but perfect love casts out fear,
because fear involves punishment, and the one who fears
is not perfected in love. We love, because He first loved us.*

1 JOHN 4:7–19 (EMPHASIS MINE.)

"Love is from God"... "everyone who loves is born of God
and knows God"... "God is love"... "the love of God was
manifested in us"... "In this is love, not that we loved God,
but that He loved us"... "the one who abides in love abides in
God." Every word and phrase was a crashing cymbal in the
empty, dark cavern of my heart. In despair and without
thinking, I blurted out "God why is it that every time I read
about your love that I get depressed?"

Immediately, He spoke with that still, small voice:
"Because you don't believe it." Those five words cut deep;
God had been saying "I love you" to me for all of my life, and
I'd been calling Him a liar, saying "no you don't"—as I
turned to worship the evil goddess of lust. The realization
that I'd been slapping God's face as He extended His hand to
me in love was excruciating.

Then, a valve in my heart that had been closed tight rotat-
ed wide open. God *did* love me, in spite of my wretched
unfaithfulness and every shameful thing I'd done. I didn't
need to do anything to deserve His love, it was there waiting
for me. An incredible force of joy blasted through my heart,
and tears streamed down my eyes. I'd found the life, love,
acceptance, and peace I'd been looking for; God was there,
and I fell in love with Him.

In John 5:39–40, Jesus is talking to the Pharisees, a group
of guys who put all of their emphasis on how good they were:

You search the Scriptures because you think that in them you have eternal life; it is these that testify about Me; and you are unwilling to come to Me so that you may have life.

The Pharisees had tons of Bible knowledge, but if you read through the New Testament you'll find they were judgmental, cold, and miserable—not unlike the average Christian sex addict. Most guys who come to our Strength in Numbers groups know plenty about God and His Word, but little of Him. In my case, some of the problem had to do with an upbringing in churches whose emphasis was on Bible knowledge and obedience to scripture, rather than knowing God.

In his book *So You Want to Be Like Christ*, Chuck Swindoll recounts the following story:

> *I'll never forget a letter I read from a graduate of Dallas Theological Seminary, where I serve as chancellor. He wrote of his gratitude for his years at our fine institution. What troubled me was that he also lamented that when he arrived, he was deeply in love with Jesus Christ, but when he left he had fallen more in love with the biblical text. For all the right reasons, our professors did their best to teach him the Scriptures, but he left loving the Bible more than he loved His Savior. To use Paul's words, "the serpent seduced him." After a few tough years in ministry, he came to realize that he needed to love Christ. I don't remember his using these precise words, but he admitted that he had to look intently at his schedule, to face the truth of his drift, and to carve out time to get back to a simple devotion to Christ.[2]*

In John 5:40 Jesus said "it is these that testify me" of His Word. The Bible tells us about and points us to Jesus; God's Word is a means to knowing Him, not the end. To have the life and love we're starved for we must come to Him, as He said.

In his book *The Pursuit of God*, AW Tozer writes:

For it is not mere words that nourish the soul, but God Himself, and unless and until the hearers find God in personal experience they are not the better for having heard the truth. The Bible is not an end in itself, but a means to bring men to an intimate and satisfying knowledge of God, that they may enter into Him, that they may delight in His presence, may taste and know the inner sweetness of the very God Himself in the core and center of their hearts.[3]

The "inner sweetness of God" is what every man and woman yearns for in the deepest recesses of their soul. Our God hunger can't be satisfied with people, sex, work, food, drugs, Bible knowledge, or anything that this life has to offer. A Christian sex addict is someone who seeks to "taste and know" the love of God deep in the "core and center of their heart" while taking a bath in the sewer of lust. It's insanity, as I know from experience.

The American Heritage Dictionary provides the following definition for the word "come": "to advance toward the speaker or toward a specified place; approach: Come to me." (Isn't it interesting how they used "come to me" as an example?) To approach Jesus we have to turn away from our sin and distorted perspectives about God, set Him as the goal in our heart, and then move toward Him.

Tozer writes:

We must simplify our approach to Him. We must strip down to essentials (and they will be found to be blessedly few). We must put away all effort to impress, and come with the guileless candor of childhood. If we do this, without doubt God will respond quickly.

When religion has said its last word, there is little that we need other than God Himself. The evil habit of seeking God—and (anything else) effectively prevents us from finding God in full revelation. In the "and" lies our great woe. If we omit the "and" we shall soon find God, and in Him we shall find that for which we have all our lives been secretly longing.[4]

It was in 1991 when I began a nine-year search for freedom from lust. At first I wondered why God waited so long to reveal that I needed to seek Him... until I thought about the motives of my heart.

I was a raging workaholic until 1997 (when I was broken by the death of our second son) so if He'd set me free from sexual sin at that time I would have continued to worship the false god of work. The Lord knew that I wanted to be free from sin so I could live life on my own terms without having to deal with guilt or shame.

One of my *ands*, as Tozer calls it, was God *and* freedom from sexual sin. When we come to God with an *and*, we tend to want the *and* more than God, which means we're in the relationship because of what God can do for us. "It's all about me" rears its ugly head again.

The Lord also allowed me to spend nine years "working the steps" and doing other things to allow me to come to the place where I was willing to set aside my pride. In part, I wanted to find freedom from sin by doing something; I wanted the glory. When God changes a life (which no man-made program can do), 100% of the glory goes to Him; we're merely recipients of His free gift of grace.

Another reason it took nine years was because I wasn't ready to surrender the control of my life to Him. As Oswald Chambers wrote: "The attitude necessary for you to come to Him is one where your will has made the determination to let go of everything and deliberately commit it all to Him." Deep down I knew the Lord would make demands on my life, and I wasn't ready to go that far. The cross by which I enter into God's presence cost Jesus everything, and for me to think I could have His life, joy, and freedom from sin and while remaining on the throne of my life was foolish, especially since my best efforts were a comic tragedy.

For some, their *"and"* is an unhealthy focus on their emotions, (I can't break free from sin until I *feel* God.) Like a drug addict in the 60's, they're in search of the ultimate emotional high that will set them free. This is little more than trying to use God as a drug, not unlike how they used sex. Joy and peace come from knowing Jesus; He must be the focus, not how we feel.

To make Jesus our only hope is to take a true leap of faith. I didn't know what God would do when I started seeking Him; I was just depending on Him to keep His promises. I sometimes think the church puts too much emphasis on programs and processes, and we forget that we serve the Almighty, Eternal, Living God for whom nothing is impossible. We're either living an adventure in faith, believing that "for God nothing is impossible," or we're floundering in the lie that "He can't handle my problems." We approach Him by leaving our physical and (often distorted) spiritual comfort zones and making the jump for His arms, trusting that He will catch us. I think the Lord loves revealing Himself in powerful ways to those who put it all on the line and go for Him.

It wasn't until I quit playing the Christian game and let go of my mask that I approached Jesus. I had to let go of all hope that I could "be good enough" if I prayed, read the Bible, or did the right Christian thing. Once I faced my brokenness (which happened after I'd tried everything and found that nothing worked) it was easy to pitch my mask and "put away all effort to impress, and come with the guileless candor of childhood," as Tozer wrote. There is no pretending or saying the right words that will impress Jesus, so we can drop our guard and come as a child.

To come to Jesus we first take our attention off of ourselves, forget our agenda, and quit pretending we're something we're not. We then pursue Him with single-minded purpose until we've found Him. Half-hearted efforts don't cut it; those who don't seek after God wholeheartedly are like Lot's wife, who yearningly turned back to look at Sodom before it got torched.

"Personal contact with Jesus changes everything," writes Chambers. In the gospel accounts, those who came to Jesus were never the same. After Mary Magdalene was set free from demonic possession she devoted her life to Him; she was the first person Jesus revealed Himself to after His resurrection (Mark 16:9). There was Zaccheus, the rich tax collector who gave half of his possessions to the poor after Jesus dined with him (Luke 19:8), the man from whom Jesus tossed the "Legion" of demons out and then begged Christ if he could follow Him (Luke 8), Peter as we discussed in the last chapter, and the Apostle Paul, a former persecutor of the church who God used mightily after Jesus appeared to Him.

What is it about Jesus that makes coming to Him so powerful and life changing? Psalms 63:3 says that "Your lovingkindness is better than life." To hear the Living God say "Peace to you; I love you; you're precious to Me" touches the deepest yearning of the heart with joy. To accept His grace is to know we are valuable and worthy to be loved, and all the lies of the past fade away. We come to know Him as He is: holy, kind, loving, beautiful, powerful, glorious, and amazing, with wisdom far deeper than we can understand. Since He sees all of us and accepts us, we find peace. Once so blessed, nothing and no one else can be as attractive, beautiful, powerful, or alluring as Christ. The desire and obsessions for porn and lust fade away, and we fall in love with Him. Without realizing it, our heart has been transformed from a concrete block into a spring of life overflowing with joy, and we can honestly say, "I love the Lord my God with all my heart, mind and soul."

You will make known to me the path of life;
In Your presence is fullness of joy;
In Your right hand there are pleasures forever.

PSALMS 16:11

It is my prayer that you will make the Living God your sole focus now, and go after Him hard until you find Him. Get away from everyone and everything else for awhile, and eliminate every distraction. Do whatever it takes.

He's promised that if you seek Him with all of your heart that you will find Him. Once you find Him, your life will never be the same.

chapter thirteen

Accepting the Gift of Grace

~

BUT GOD, BEING RICH IN MERCY, BECAUSE OF HIS GREAT LOVE WITH
WHICH HE LOVED US, EVEN WHEN WE WERE DEAD IN OUR TRANS-
GRESSIONS, MADE US ALIVE TOGETHER WITH CHRIST (BY GRACE YOU
HAVE BEEN SAVED), AND RAISED US UP WITH HIM, AND SEATED US
WITH HIM IN THE HEAVENLY PLACES IN CHRIST JESUS, SO THAT IN
THE AGES TO COME HE MIGHT SHOW THE SURPASSING RICHES OF HIS
GRACE IN KINDNESS TOWARD US IN CHRIST JESUS. FOR BY GRACE YOU
HAVE BEEN SAVED THROUGH FAITH; AND THAT NOT OF YOURSELVES,
IT IS THE GIFT OF GOD; NOT AS A RESULT OF WORKS, SO THAT NO
ONE MAY BOAST. FOR WE ARE HIS WORKMANSHIP, CREATED IN
CHRIST JESUS FOR GOOD WORKS, WHICH GOD PREPARED BEFORE-
HAND SO THAT WE WOULD WALK IN THEM.

Ephesians 2:4–10

The opening minutes of *Les Miserables*, the 1998 film
adaptation of Victor Hugo's book of the same name,
serves up one of the most poignant scenes of grace I've ever
seen.[1] Set in 19th century France, the film opens as Jean
Valjean (pronounced John Valjohn) a hardened criminal

who'd just been released from prison is lying on a park bench late at night, trying to go to sleep. Valjean is filthy, and dressed in worn out clothes.

After an old woman points him to a nearby church, Valjean knocks on the door, which is opened by a priest. Valjean shows his passport, which identifies him as a convict, and curtly asks the priest if he might spare any food. To Valjean's surprise, the priest warmly invites him in for dinner and a room for the night. Nineteen years of harsh treatment in chains have conditioned Valjean to expect rejection and cruelty, not kindness, and he refuses to believe that the priest will take him in. He reiterates that he's a convict to the priest—twice—but the offer for food and lodging still stands.

In spite of the priest's hospitality, Valjean is more scorning than thankful. As he wolfs down his food, Valjean makes a sarcastic remark about murder being his crime—and that he could do the same to the priest. (He later reveals that he received his long prison term because of stealing food.) When the priest makes a remark about man's unjustness in relation to the harsh life Valjean has endured, Valjean bitterly accuses God of being the same.

Later that night after everyone is asleep, Valjean gets up and begins piling the priest's silverware into a large cloth bag. Awakened by the noise, the priest walks into the room—and comes face to face with the man who is now stealing from him. With a look of scorn, Valjean slugs the priest's face so hard that he's knocked unconscious, and then flees the church, clutching the bag of silverware.

The next morning, as the priest is gardening with Madame Gilot, the police arrive with Valjean and the sack of silverware in hand. After one of the officers asks the priest if he had given Valjean the bag of silverware, the priest, who's sporting a black eye courtesy of his former houseguest, tells them he did indeed give the silverware to Valjean—and then sends a shocked Madame Gilot into the house to fetch their silver candlesticks (which are worth at least 2,000 francs) to give to Valjean.

After Madame Gilot reappears with the candlesticks, the priest takes them, and asks her to bring the police officers inside for some wine. As she escorts the officers into the church, the priest places the candlesticks in the bag of silverware, and then thrusts it into the arms of Valjean, who is now more bewildered than ever.

Valjean stands there, frozen, clutching a bag of silverware worth thousands of francs, given to him by the man who he'd beaten just hours ago. A man, who, to Valjean's shame, has showed him nothing but kindness from the moment he met him. A pained look comes over Valjean's face; accepting love is hard for one who's been trained to expect rejection and cruelty. He now has a simple choice to make: he can drop the cloth bag and refuse the priest's generosity and kindness, or he can accept it.

It is the acceptance of this gift that forever changes the former convict's life. In the rest of the movie we see a new Valjean; a man of compassion who freely gives the same gifts of mercy that he's received to others.

For by grace you have been saved through faith;
and that not of yourselves, it is the gift of God.

EPHESIANS 2:8

But by the grace of God I am what I am, and His grace toward
me did not prove vain; but I labored even more than all of them,
yet not I, but the grace of God with me.

1 CORINTHIANS 15:10

I have been in Jean Valjean's shoes. Like the former convict, I was spiritually filthy, dispirited and hardened, and yet, Jesus invited me to come to Him. In spite of His kindness (and even while I was a Christian), I looked the Lord in the eye, and struck Him by turning to porn, lust, or promiscuity.

"You're not enough for me, Jesus, I want lust instead." I was Jean Valjean and Peter all rolled up into one; I might as well have said, "I do not know the man" (Matthew 26:72).

In spite of how I treated Him, the Lord continued packing a bag full of His vessels of grace for me—a bag that, unlike Valjean, I refused to accept. Years ago, during a time when I was traveling often and binging on porn in hotel rooms, the words "Beloved of the Lord" were brought to my mind repeatedly over a number of weeks. "These words can't be for me; they can't be from God," I thought. "It must be my imagination." I expected judgment and wrath from the Lord, not love.

Like Valjean, we expect God's love to be as small, shallow, distorted by false motives, and performance-based as the love we've encountered from other broken men and women. Maybe we think He will shame, abuse, or condemn us for our faults.

God's love is nothing like that of man. If the priest tried to give Valjean the sack of valuables in four separate instances and got decked every time, what are the chances he would have kept trying? If a man has multiple affairs on his wife, how much pain and betrayal can she take before she leaves? I carried on a love affair with lust and sex for *years*, and yet the Lord kept calling me, and inviting me in; there were times when I'd binge on porn just minutes after talking with Him. In spite of the ways we abuse Him, the Lord keeps knocking on the door of our heart.

> *"For My thoughts are not your thoughts,*
> *Nor are your ways My ways," declares the Lord.*
>
> ISAIAH 55:8

> *Just as the Father has loved Me,*
> *I have also loved you; abide in My love.*
>
> JOHN 15:9

But God, being rich in mercy, because of His great love
with which He loved us, even when we were dead in our
transgressions, made us alive together with Christ (by grace
you have been saved), and raised us up with Him, and seated
us with Him in the heavenly places in Christ Jesus, so that in
the ages to come He might show the surpassing riches of His
grace in kindness toward us in Christ Jesus.

EPHESIANS 2:4–7

The passage above from Ephesians reveals a God Who loves even when we are striking, denying, and running away from Him. "For the Son of Man has come to seek and to save that which was lost" (Luke 19:10); He intentionally seeks the Jean Valjeans of this world in order to win their hearts, even as they eye Him with contempt. This is the "great love that He loves us with."

But God demonstrates His own love toward us,
in that while we were yet sinners, Christ died for us.

ROMANS 5:8

I want you to notice that there isn't a list of names of persons whom God doesn't love, namely yours, in Ephesians 2:4. The text doesn't say "But God, being rich in mercy, because of His great love with which He loved everyone but (fill in the blank with your name)…." His grace is yours for the taking.

There's no gray zone when it comes to the love of God. Either His Word is true, and He loves you with the "great love" He says He does… or He doesn't and it's all a lie. Just as Jean Valjean had a choice whether he would accept or refuse the bag of tableware from the priest, you have a choice as to whether you will receive the love of God, or refuse it.

Sadly, there are many who choose the latter, which is why hell has no shortage of occupants. Some are deceived by lies, while others intentionally choose themselves, people, pleasure, money, or other things over God's love. Some try to pretend He doesn't exist, which, to me, takes a lot more faith than believing in Almighty God.

If you believe that the Lord is the creator of the Universe and His words are true, then the only conclusion you can come to is that He loves you, regardless of your past, what you've done, or what others have said.

> *For God so loved the world, that He gave His only*
> *begotten Son, that whoever believes in Him*
> *shall not perish, but have eternal life.*
>
> JOHN 3:16

> *For the word of the cross is foolishness to those who are*
> *perishing, but to us who are being saved it is the power of God.*
>
> 1 CORINTHIANS 1:18

Jesus wasn't messing around when He went to the cross; can you picture Him taking the torture He did because He loved us *only a little*? Or because He wanted to be a nice God that day? Most Christians have no idea how powerful Jesus' act on the cross really was; all of God's love, power and mercy were poured out through His death and made available to us. We receive the Holy Spirit because of the cross (Acts 2:38); it was His Spirit saying "Beloved of the Lord" to me. (Satan, I am sure, has no motive to say such a thing.) We receive the power to overcome sin from the cross (1 Peter 2:24), and, we are adopted into the family of God as His beloved children because of it:

> *See how great a love the Father has bestowed on us, that we*
> *would be called children of God; and such we are.*
>
> 1 JOHN 3:1

Because of the cross, we have been given a treasure trove of spiritual blessings...

Blessed be the God and Father of our Lord Jesus Christ,
who has blessed us with every spiritual blessing
in the heavenly places in Christ.

EPHESIANS 1:3

Grace and peace be multiplied to you in the knowledge
of God and Jesus our Lord, as His divine power has given
us all things that pertain to life and godliness, through
the knowledge of Him who called us by His glory and virtue,
by which have been given to us exceedingly great
and precious promises, that through these you may be
partakers of the divine nature, having escaped the
corruption that is in the world through lust.

2 PETER 1:2–4

Many Christians are keeping themselves trapped in shame and despair, as I did, because they won't allow the Son of God to hold them, love them, and care for them. When He whispers "Beloved of the Lord," they push Him away, thinking He can't be saying such words to them. What they don't realize is that they're rejecting all the power and love of God that they've been seeking all of their life.

God the Father sent His Son to be butchered for you and me because He is love (1 John 4:8), and He wants you to receive that glowing bag of blessings and love He's thrust in your chest. Whether you realize it or not, you're already surrounded and submerged by His grace. Even as you're reading this book, He's calling to you, inviting you in.

For of His fullness we have all received, and grace upon grace.
For the Law was given through Moses; grace and truth were
realized through Jesus Christ.

JOHN 1:16–17

So how do we receive the gift of His grace? First, we rarely receive presents from persons we don't know, which means first building a relationship with God until we know we can trust Him. From God of Grace (chapter 12) and what we've discussed in this chapter, we know that the Lord is our friend.

No longer do I call you slaves, for the slave does
not know what his master is doing; but I have called you
friends, for all things that I have heard from
My Father I have made known to you.

JOHN 15:15

We are *His* true friends if we've made the decision to forsake lust and sexual sin and make Him the Lord of our life…

and whatever we ask we receive from Him,
because we keep His commandments
and do the things that are pleasing in His sight.

1 JOHN 3:22

…and if we believe He is the God of Grace He says He is:

And without faith it is impossible to please Him,
for he who comes to God must believe that He is
and that He is a rewarder of those who seek Him.

HEBREW 11:6

Then, we must approach the person who wishes to give us the gift, as was discussed in the last chapter, ("Come to me so that you may have life," John 5:40.) Our friends don't lob gifts to us from afar, especially if it's a heavy cloth bag filled with expensive silverware and other precious items. We must approach them so we can receive the gift.

When we're face-to-face with the Living God and He's pressing a huge bag of grace in on us, we don't question the gift, whether we're worthy of it, or why He wants to give it to us. We wouldn't say, "Wait here for me, Lord; I need to go study the Bible first so I can get my theology straight. I'll get back to you when I get it." Only a fool would dare insult the Creator of the Universe by saying, "I'll accept your gifts of love after you tell me how I can earn them."

The definition for the word receive is "to take or acquire something given, offered, or transmitted." What Jesus offers, *we can take!* Like a child on Christmas morning, we can grab the gift and rip it open! We can celebrate by dancing around the room with joy, and shout aloud with praise and thanksgiving for that which is now ours to keep forever. We can weep for joy because the Most Powerful Being in the Universe is a God of light, love, and peace, and we can enjoy sweet communion with Him for the rest of our earthly life, and into eternity. There is no more striving to earn the gift, no more shame, no more listening to Satan's lies that we've sinned too much for God to love us—and no need for the pathetic counterfeit of lust. The love of God is, has been, and always will be, ours to keep (Romans 8:35).

> *Keep yourselves in the love of God, waiting anxiously*
> *for the mercy of our Lord Jesus Christ to eternal life.*
>
> JUDE 1:21

Receiving God's love isn't a one time event; we're invited to keep going back to Him for more for the rest of our life, and what a blessing it is to do so.

It was September of 2003, and I was burned out. We had endured financial stress for two years due to a failing business that was eventually sold at a loss, and had needed to sell our house to pay off some debts. We found a buyer in late July, and he gave us two weeks to pack up and move out. By the time we made the mad dash to pack up and then move out on one of the hottest days of the year, I was drained of all energy and enthusiasm.

I knew I needed some time to get my batteries recharged with the Lord, but wasn't able to take a vacation. The new business I'd started was growing, and demanded my attention, and our kids were back in school; life was moving forward and I had to keep up.

I had to make a business trip to Southern California, and decided to stay the weekend alone in a city that few would choose—Borrego Springs.

Borrego Springs is a small, isolated desert town, three hours' drive southeast of Los Angeles, in the Anza-Borrego Desert State Park. There are no fast food restaurants, no freeways, a few stoplights, and a population of about 2,500... in the non-summer months, that is. From July through September, when the temperatures hit 110 + degrees, some of the locals vacate the city for cooler temperatures, and a number of the stores are closed. The town is set in a valley enclosed from the west by dry, rocky hills; the desert floor of which is landscaped with an occasional palm tree, green cactus, and floating brown tumbleweeds.

My hotel, a desert resort, was set back from the hills a couple of miles. Having been there before, I knew there was a small grove of palm trees about a 10 minute walk from the hotel towards the hills, and it was here where I planned to meet with the Lord.

I arrived at the hotel on a Friday night, and woke up early Saturday morning, eager to make my way to the palm grove. I grabbed my Bible, and as I was starting to leave the room, three words broke through: "Bring a pen." I was in a hurry to reach my destination and ignored it, shut the door, and started walking.

But those same words came back again: *"Bring a pen."* This time, I got the point that the Lord wanted me to record something He had to say. I ran back in the room and grabbed a pen.

There are few places suited for seeking God like the desert. Here there is none of the din, clamor and distractions that are found in the city; only rugged terrain, scorching temperature, and silence that is as thick as the heat. Quiet solitude calms, deepens and strengthens a man's heart, opening the door for intimate communion with the Living God. The Lord trained Moses in the wilderness for 40 years, raised John the Baptist there, and sent Jesus into it for 40 days prior to the start of His earthly ministry. We do our best listening and receiving in silence.

In quietness and trust is your strength.

ISAIAH 30:15

The grove is made up of a collection of seven large desert palm trees, each which are 12 to 15 feet tall. The wide green fronds at the top of each tree float gently like silent fans, providing shade for any visitors who make use of the picnic bench that the Department of Park and Recreation has placed there for visitors.

After taking a few moments to breathe in the quiet serenity of the environment around me, I opened my Bible, hunted around in the Psalms, and settled in with chapter 63. The third verse stood out: "Because your lovingkindness is better than life, my lips shall praise you."

I turned the implication of those words over in my mind; the Psalmist was saying that God's love is better than being alive and all that goes with it: success in work or ministry, money, sex, people, or having fun. Wanting to know more about this incredible love, I quickly scanned the surrounding chapters, and found 59:10: "My God in His lovingkindess will meet me." Verse 16 added: "I shall joyfully sing of Thy lovingkindness in the morning."

Then, I had a strong sense I wasn't alone, and His voice broke through again: "I have made you and I love you; you are dear to me."

"Is that you Lord?" I wondered aloud. Could He really be speaking such wonderful words to me? Or was this just something I was making up in my head?

He pressed in deeper: "I love you Mike."

At hearing this, my dry, crusty heart melted into a burst of joy; tears streamed down my face as I was instantly filled to overflowing with light, love, and peace. It felt like Heaven. I spent several minutes singing quiet praises to the Lord, thanking Him for the precious gift of His presence that morning. His love *is* better than life, and His blazing grace is truly amazing; He presses in even when I'm ignoring Him, distracted, or doubting.

I knew now what the pen was for, and quickly wrote in a blank page at the back of my Bible the verses I'd read in Psalms that morning, along with the words the Lord had spoken to me. At the bottom of the page I wrote "9-20-03, Borrego Springs."

I think the Lord had me grab a pen that morning not just for me, but also for you, because I believe He wants to meet with *you*, and shower *you* with this love that is better than life.

I shall finish this book here, in hopes that you will approach Him in a quiet place, and receive it. There is no greater blessing than that which comes from being in the Presence of the Living God.

> *...and hope does not disappoint, because the love*
> *of God has been poured out within our hearts*
> *through the Holy Spirit who was given to us.*
>
> ROMANS 5:5

*But to each one of us grace was given
according to the measure of Christ's gift.*

EPHESIANS 4:7

*You will make known to me the path of life;
In Your presence is fullness of joy;
in Your right hand there are pleasures forever.*

PSALMS 16:11

The Little Boy

an allegory

In his early years, The Little Boy was a happy kid, with a fun, adventurous spirit. He loved playing with his army toys and pretending to be the hero who saved the day. He would imagine himself as Rambo, fearless, determined, and with big biceps, able to jump into battle at a moment's notice against overwhelming odds and win. Or he'd picture himself as Braveheart, a leader whose courage and integrity was admired by both men and women. Yes sir, that's the kind of man The Little Boy wanted to be. He would paint his face blue and dash around the backyard, slashing at bushes and trees with his toy sword, taking on imaginary foes in desperate battle.

Most of all, The Little Boy wanted to be like his daddy; he was everything The Little Boy wanted to be: smart, strong and tough. He was proud of his daddy, and would boast to other little boys that his daddy could whip theirs. He loved it when they would wrestle and laugh together or talk about men stuff… when his daddy was home, that is. His daddy traveled a lot for his job, and was often gone. It made The Little Boy sad that he couldn't have more time with him.

But The Little Boy noticed that other little boys didn't get sad; they were too rough 'n rowdy to feel things like that, so he decided to be a rough 'n rowdy boy too. Although they said and did things his parents had told him not to, which got him into trouble, it made him feel good when the other boys told him how cool he was.

One day, his mommy and daddy had to go somewhere, and they left him and his little sister with Uncle Frank to stay the night at his house. The Little Boy had always thought Uncle Frank was weird; his uncle was quiet, and every once in a while he would see Uncle Frank looking at him in a strange way that made him feel uncomfortable.

But that night, Uncle Frank seemed happy; they watched fun movies together and had popcorn, and he let them stay up for awhile. When it got late, Uncle Frank put his little sister to bed first, in a guest bedroom in the house. Then Uncle Frank brought The Little Boy into his bedroom... and did some horrible things to him... that involved touching The Little Boy's private parts.

Afterwards, The Little Boy was so sick that he threw up; he wanted to run away, but was too afraid. "If you tell anyone what happened," Uncle Frank told him, "I'll do this to you again." The Little Boy promised he wouldn't say a word.

Over the next few years, The Little Boy started to change. Some days he got angry for no reason; on others, he cried a lot. He wanted to tell his daddy what happened so he could pound Uncle Frank, but his daddy was traveling even more. His mommy and daddy fought a lot, too. The Little Boy was now afraid of being touched by other people. He hated family get-togethers, because Aunt Susie, who had to hug and kiss everyone, was always there. Some nights, he had nightmares about what happened with Uncle Frank; when this happened he often woke up shivering in fear.

One day a few years later, The Little Boy was at Jimmie's house. Jimmie was another rough 'n rowdy boy, and he and The Little Boy hung out together a lot. Jimmie took The Little Boy to a hiding place in his room, and showed The Little Boy a collection of magazines he had; magazines with lots of shocking pictures of little girls. Although The Little Boy instinctively knew these magazines were bad, the pictures excited him. "Go on, take one home," laughed Jimmie. "I have plenty more."

The Little Boy took the magazine home, and looked at it. He looked at it a lot. He remembered what Uncle Frank did to him, and how it felt, and did it to himself. "This is fun," The Little Boy thought; soon, he had his own hidden collection of magazines, just like Jimmie.

One day The Little Boy's mommy and daddy started going to church. They'd recently heard about someone named Jesus, and going to church seemed to be what people did who wanted to know more about Him. In church, The Little Boy learned that Jesus is God, and that He loves him and died on the cross for him. He heard that bad people go to hell, and that Christians, people who love Jesus, go to Heaven. The Little Boy didn't want to go to hell, so he decided to become a Christian; immediately, something strange happened inside. The Little Boy found that he didn't want to be rough 'n rowdy anymore; he wanted to please Jesus.

The Little Boy went to several churches over the years with his parents, and noticed that the pastors said different things about God. One pastor screamed "if you sin a lot you will go to hell!" which scared The Little Boy, so he started trying his best to be good. Another said "you need to learn everything in the Bible and do what it says so you can please God." A third pastor said "God loves you" a lot. The Little Boy liked to hear this, but didn't always feel like God loved him, especially after he looked at his magazines. "Besides, if God loves me, why did He let Uncle Frank do those things to me," he wondered.

One day at church, The Little Boy met a pretty Little Girl in a blue dress. This Little Girl was special; she knocked him out like no other little girl had before. He loved everything about her—how she looked, talked and thought. When they were together, he was happy, and didn't want to leave her. Soon, they became best friends.

Growing up, The Little Girl loved to dance. A few years back, when her school was putting on a play, she was to be the main character. This play meant everything to The Little Girl; she practiced her moves two hours each day in the months leading up to it. She wanted that night to be perfect.

The day before the play, her mommy took her to a store to buy a beautiful, frilly white dress and new shoes, just for the play. "I can't wait for my daddy to see me in this dress," she thought, as she looked at her image in the mirror at the store. He would be so proud. When they arrived home, they saw there was a note on the kitchen counter. Her mommy started crying as she read it. "He left us," she said. The Little Girl's daddy had left them for another mommy, who had two other little girls. Brokenhearted, The Little Girl never wore that dress again, neither did she participate in the play; she told the school she was too sick to dance, and another little girl took her part.

It wasn't long before The Little Girl and The Little Boy decided to become Best Friends for Life. Both of them were excited; now they would be loved by someone who wouldn't hurt them. In the excitement of getting married, The Little Boy threw his collection of magazines in the trash; he wouldn't need them now that he had his Little Girl.

For the first few months, their marriage was a lot of fun; they laughed, kissed and hugged each other a lot; being Best Friends for Life was great. But then, something started going wrong; The Little Boy started feeling like he did before they were Best Friends for Life—angry, scared, and like he wanted to cry a lot. He stopped talking to his Little Girl as before, and they didn't kiss as much. The Little Girl felt hurt, and unloved, and started pushing her Little Boy to talk and tell her what was wrong. Problem was, the more she pushed him, the more scared he got, and they ended up fighting a lot.

One day, while The Little Girl was away at the store, The Little Boy discovered he could look at pictures like those that were in his old magazine collection by using his computer to get on the Internet. He remembered how good this used to make him feel; "this is the only safe way I can be loved," he told himself. He started looking at the pictures of other little girls on the computer and touching himself often, sneaking out to their computer room after his Little Girl had gone to sleep, or when she was out running errands.

Late one night, The Little Girl woke up after The Little Boy had left their room to get on the computer. Puzzled by his absence, she walked into their computer room, and was horrified to see her Little Boy touching himself as he was looking at pictures of other little girls on their computer. She couldn't believe what her Best Friend for Life was doing, and started crying.

The Little Boy was embarrassed, and felt awful; how could he have hurt His Little Girl this way? "I'll never do it again, I'm sorry," he boldly promised her. The Little Girl wanted to trust her Little Boy more than anything; although she was deeply hurt, she believed him and agreed to move on.

In the weeks that followed, the pictures from those images keep coming back to The Little Boy's mind, and he eventually broke his promise to The Little Girl. "It'll be okay as long as she doesn't find out," he thought. "What she doesn't know won't hurt her." She asked him from time to time if he was still looking at the pictures, but he always lied, not wanting to hurt her again.

Even though her Little Boy said he wasn't looking at the pictures anymore, there was something about the way he acted that didn't feel right to The Little Girl. He didn't laugh much anymore, and was quiet a lot; he rarely kissed her. When she asked him if everything was okay, he got angry and defensive, as if he was irritated that she could even ask him this question. Even though he said nothing was wrong, their friendship seemed to be dying.

One day a few months later, as The Little Girl was typing a letter on their computer at home, she hit a key by mistake— and was horrified when a shocking picture of another little girl popped up to the screen. Hoping this was an isolated incident, she called one of her friends, who told her how to find where pictures are stored on the computer—and was stunned to find hundreds more. From the dates on the files, it appeared that her Little Boy had been looking at pictures of other little girls *every day.* "How could I have believed him all this time!?" she asked herself, through tears of anger and hurt.

This was too much for her to take; she quickly wrote a note that said: "You've hurt me too much, and I can't trust you. I'm sorry, but I can't be your Best Friend for Life anymore." She packed her bags, and left their home.

Later that evening, The Little Boy was puzzled to come home to a dark house. "Usually she leaves a light on, what's going…" and then he saw her note. "*Oh no! What have I done?*" he screamed. His first instinct was to rush to the computer and look at more of those pictures so he could feel better and forget about his loneliness… but then, he realized

"This junk is the reason why I lost my Little Girl... I don't want it anymore; I want her." In a panic, he called his Little Girl at her Mommy's house and promised to be good, but she refused to listen. "You've lied to me too many times; I can't trust you again with my heart," she said, and hung up.

That night, The Little Boy cried more than he had at any other time in his life. He thought about God and all the things he'd heard said at church. He knew what the Bible said, but had disobeyed it for years; "maybe I've sinned so much I'm going to hell," he wondered. "Maybe Jesus doesn't love me anymore."

"God, I've made a mess of my life and I don't know what to do; if you're there, please help me," he prayed. The Little Boy was so sick from sadness that he felt like he wanted to throw up. Finally, late at night, he fell asleep.

As the Little Boy is sleeping, Jesus appears to him in a dream; he and Jesus are standing outside of a house that looks strangely familiar...

Jesus is wearing a bright white robe; light seems to emanate from Him. There is a look of compassion in His eyes, as He asks the Little Boy: "Will you let me heal you?" Although the Little Boy is scared, the look on Jesus' face puts him at ease.

"I think so. What do I have to do?"

"Enter this house with Me."

Suddenly, the Little Boy remembers whose house they're standing in front of—it's Uncle Frank's.

"*I can't go in there... I can't*," the Little Boy says, in a terrified whisper.

"The choice is yours. You can stay where you are, if you like, but this will be as good as your life will get."

The Little Boy thinks back to where his actions had taken him, and how he'd lost his Little Girl.

"Okay."

In an instant, the Little Boy and Jesus are standing in Uncle Frank's bedroom, the place where those horrible things were done to the Little Boy. He feels sick to his stomach… and angry. He hates Uncle Frank. "*Why*?" he asks. "Jesus, why did you let this happen to me??"

Jesus looks at him with a steady gaze: "Will knowing why make a difference?" He asks softy.

"I…." and then, the Little Boy realizes that Jesus is right; knowing "why" can't change what happened. A sense of utter hopelessness washes over him, and the Little Boy starts to cry.

Jesus extends his right hand out to him, and says:

"I love you, my child."

Upon hearing this, the Little Boy rushes into Jesus arms and lets it all out; years of pain, shame, and sorrow are poured out with deep, heaving sobs. As he allows Jesus to comfort him, the warmth of God's love breaks into his heart, healing the Little Boy's heart. God *does* love him, just as the Bible says.

"My Child, you've been in this room all of your life, and it's kept you trapped in pain and sin. Are you ready to leave it?"

"Yes, Lord!"

"To leave this room, you must forgive your uncle."

The Little Boy hesitated for a moment; this was unexpected. Uncle Frank doesn't deserve forgiveness; heck, he'd never even asked for it. And yet, the joy in the Little Boy's heart is too good to mess up with bitterness any longer; what further use would his anger serve?

"I forgive Uncle Frank," the Little Boy says firmly.

Jesus smiles: "You must never return to that room again."

Instantly, the Little Boy finds that he and Jesus are back in the living room of his home. The only light in the house comes from Jesus; all the lights in the house are still off. "Can I have my Little Girl back now?" the Little Boy asks.

"It's up to her. If she won't allow me to heal her as you've done, she may not come back. There are many little girls who've been hurt by their little boys who don't return. No matter what happens, I must be your First Best Friend now, not the Little Girl. If she should return to you again, you must resolve to let her into your heart on a consistent basis to keep your relationship alive. She wants you, not the breadcrumbs of your life. Will you trust Me, no matter what happens?"

After hours of crying at her mommy's house, the Little Girl has made up her mind; she's not going back to her Little Boy. "Maybe the Little Boy I first met never existed," she wonders. She feels hard, cold, and empty inside. "I won't let anyone hurt me like that again," she promises herself.

That night, Jesus appears to her in a dream; He and the Little Girl are standing outside the house where she grew up.

"Will you let me heal you?" He asks.

"Heal *me*? From *what*?"

Jesus is silent; He merely looks at her with an intense, yet compassionate gaze that melts her heart like a wax candle.

"Okay," she says.

Suddenly, they are in the kitchen, standing in front of the counter—and there's a note on it; the one her daddy wrote when he left.

"Where have you been all of my life?" the Little Girl asks Jesus… "Why did my father leave us? And why did you give me a Little Boy who looks at pictures of other little girls??"

Softly, Jesus repeats his original question: "Will you let me heal you?"

"*Why isn't He answering my questions?*" she wonders, as she nods again.

There's a long rectangular box sitting on the kitchen counter. Jesus walks up to it, takes it, and then hands it to the

Little Girl. In the box is the dress her mother had bought her for the dance.

"Will you dance for me?" Jesus asks.

The Little Girl can't believe what she just heard; the King of the Universe is inviting her to dance for Him.

"Okay," she whispers, trying to hold back tears.

Suddenly, they are in a school auditorium. The Little Girl is wearing the white dress and shoes that her mommy bought her, and is standing center stage; all lights are on her. There are many persons in the crowd, but it's dark and she can't make out their faces, except for one. There, seated in the center of the front row, is Jesus, who's smiling at her like a proud father.

Music starts playing, and the Little Girl dances, like she's never danced before; her timing is perfect, her moves are crisp. As she dances, she can't take her eyes off of Jesus; He's watching her every move with interest.

A few minutes later, the Little Girl finishes her dance, and there is thunderous applause; the lights come on, and she's sees that the auditorium is packed with angels. As she stands there, stunned, Jesus stands up, walks up to her, and embraces her; the Little Girl collapses to the floor, sobbing, pouring out the pain of her life to Him. After every tear is cried out, warmth spreads through her heart, and there is joy where anger and sorrow had been. For the first time in her life, she knows she is loved.

"My daughter, will you forgive your father for leaving you?"

"Yes, Lord," the Little Girl responds eagerly.

"Will you forgive the Little Boy?"

This wasn't easy. He'd hurt her like no one else had.

"Does forgiving him mean I have to go back to him?"

"No, that choice is yours. But if you choose not to release him, you will keep your heart poisoned with bitterness."

The Little Girl thought about it for a few seconds, and then, quietly, says, "Yes, I forgive him. But Jesus, I can't go back to the Little Boy if he's going to hurt me like that again. Will you heal Him like you healed me?"

"Every little boy has to choose to let Me heal Him; there are many who don't. If you want to know the answer to this, go and ask him. If you choose to stay, you will need to accept him as he is to make the relationship work. I have made him like he is for a purpose, and your role will be to build him up into My purpose."

Two weeks later, it's 6:00 at night, and the Little Boy is home, alone. Although he hasn't heard from the Little Girl since she left, he's determined to trust Jesus no matter what happens.

There's a knock at the door… the Little Boy opens it, and is amazed at the sight before him. There, standing at the doorway, is his Little Girl, wearing a white dress. She looks like an angel; her hair is made up in a way he's never seen before, and a thin gold necklace with a cross adorns her neck. The Little Boy steps backward, until his legs hit the bottom of the couch and he falls onto it… he doesn't know what to say, and anything he might say feels like it couldn't be enough.

The Little Girl steps in, closes the door, and sits at the other end of the couch. Both of them look at each other without speaking for several minutes.

Finally, the Little Boy musters up the courage to speak:
"I'm sorry."
The Little Girl nods…
"I've met Jesus!" he says.
"You *have*?" she asks. "So have I!"
Slowly, they take each other's hand…
…and Jesus smiles.

The Wife's Path

~~

There are many weeks when I get more emails from wives who are asking how to cope with their husband's betrayal than I do from the men. A wife suffers an immense amount of pain and needs as much help recovering from her husbands' infidelity as he does in breaking free from it.

A few years back, I asked Michelle to write a letter describing how my struggle with sexual sin affected her. The following is what she wrote:

At the time, things were a bit hazy; I was young and didn't know what to think of everything. It really flared my insecurities. I measured myself up to other women "in your eyes." I was always trying to see what you'd find more attractive in others—where my flaws were. The beginning of our marriage was the worst. My insecurities plus your addiction equaled disaster.

I watched porn movies a few times out of curiosity to see where I was lacking in bed. In a way it was self-torture. "I wasn't good enough," "I didn't measure up." What was it that you were looking at or drawn to that I couldn't fill? I was constantly looking at women (probably more than you) to see if you'd notice her smaller waist, her bigger chest, her whatever.

I've gotten better about not letting it be "my fault." If you ever decide to go down that road again and self destruct, it isn't going to be my fault. It would affect me, yes, but not like 12 years ago.

Your sex addiction ruined the little bit of self-esteem I had back then, and there wasn't much of it to begin with. It put me on guard for everything—I was afraid that if I weren't "perfect" (whatever that is) you'd leave or stray. I made you my everything, which was wrong, and when you cheated on me with a prostitute in 1991, it devastated me.

Today I still struggle with insecurity; I'm paranoid about any pictures that might be in something we might get in the mail, or even a magazine I might want to read. It's not that I think you're going to go back to where you were, but that you'll see in that picture what you don't have in me.

The process of healing from a spouse's adultery or porn addiction is difficult, often painful, and one that takes time. Because God is in the restoration business, He is able to heal a woman's heart and restore her marriage. Often, this new relationship is stronger than the old one. I'll use some of the points my wife brought up in her letter as a guide for some of the issues we'll examine.

1. Your husband's porn/sex addiction is not your fault.

You could be a 20-year-old with the perfect body who gives her husband all the sex he wanted, and it still wouldn't "fix" his struggle with sexual sin. Sexual addiction is a counterfeit method of dealing with the emptiness, pain, and loneliness in a man's heart; the search for God's love in the wrong place. Sex can't fill an empty heart with the love of God, and neither can you; his choice to commit adultery by lusting in his mind, using porn or having sex with another person isn't something you caused or can resolve—*no matter what he says.*

Some guys try to use "if you were only giving me more sex I wouldn't be this way" as a smoke screen. If your husband throws this line at you, *call him on it*; never allow him to pin his choice to serve the god of lust on you.

If your husband is deep in sexual addiction, he will probably be defensive, immersed in self-absorption, and obsessed with protecting his "precious," which means he may try to do anything to avoid accepting responsibility for his sin. 100% of the blame for his decision to worship the false goddess of lust lies on his shoulders; never allow your husband to put a guilt trip on you.

> *But each one is tempted when he is*
> *carried away and enticed by his own lust.*
>
> JAMES 1:14

2. Don't allow your husband to treat you like a prostitute.

Wives allow their husbands to treat them like a whore when they allow them to indulge in sexual sin unabated and unchallenged. When you were engaged, if your groom-to-be had said "I'm going to masturbate to pictures of other naked women at least once a week, and might have an affair or two while we're married," you probably wouldn't have walked down the aisle with him.

You're a precious daughter of God, not a trophy for his bookshelf to be dusted off and used when he pleases.

> *An excellent wife, who can find?*
> *For her worth is far above jewels.*
>
> PROVERBS 31:10

If your husband is persisting in porn or sex addiction, you must draw a line in the sand with him: "it's me or porn... or we need to talk about separation." I know this sounds harsh, but if you don't take a tough stand then you're giving him permission to continue in sin (also known as enabling). Separation is a valid alternative that shows zero tolerance for any forms of adultery, while avoiding the nuclear destruction of divorce. Sadly, many Christian men won't face how damaging their addiction to sexual sin is until their wives say "no more." The majority of men who come to our group for the first time are there because their wives caught them and demanded that they get help.

You should accept nothing less from your husband than an all-out commitment to do whatever it takes, *immediately*, to break free from lust. If he isn't going all out then he won't get better; refusing to get help also means he's still trying to hold onto the adulteress of lust.

Most sex addicts are professional liars, which means his actions are your only proof he's serious about divorcing lust, not his words. "Serious" is meeting with an accountability group or partner once a week, removing his stumbling blocks from your home (i.e., installing accountability software such as Covenant Eyes, or shutting off Internet or TV service if necessary) and facing the heart issues that drove him to lust.

Confrontation is hard, but it saves your family. It's a terrifying prospect for a man to talk about his sexual sin, especially when it involves masturbating to porn. Some men will resort to outbursts of anger and hollow accusations ("you're not giving me enough sex") to deflect attention away from the core issue. If he tries "bait and switch" on you, don't bite; stay focused on his actions.

If you need to confront your husband, I suggest that you take several days and pray first. If possible, ask some of your friends to do the same. Ask the Lord to soften your husband's heart and prepare him to face the truth, and ask for His guidance in the proper timing and approach. Confrontation is best done in a spirit of love, not attack; do your best to speak the truth in love.

If he won't listen to what you have to say, you have two choices; pack up or ask him to leave, or, you might consider asking some Christian men who know him to do an intervention.

Your marriage and your children are at stake in this battle; if your husband is acting out with porn, he's corrupting your home with evil. Satan has used many a fathers' porn stash to introduce their children to this wicked media; I hear stories all the time from men whose first exposure to porn came from their father. Every day you put off confronting him is another day your family is at risk.

Although confronting your best friend is difficult and painful, I can tell you that I've heard many a man say that getting caught was the best thing that happened to them; it forced them out of hiding and onto the path to freedom.

3. Trust your instincts.

My experience has been that women sense when their husbands are messing with porn or sex addiction long before they know it cognitively. Women are gifted with a sixth sense that men lack; if your heart's telling you that something's wrong with your husband (and it's not your insecurity talking), then chances are you're right. The warning signs are emotional withdrawal, isolation, lack of (or too much) interest in sex, defensiveness, a hard, critical spirit, and staying up late to "work" on the computer or watch TV. Follow your instinct up with prayer, and ask the One who brings every secret to the light to do so with your husband.

The king answered Daniel and said, "Surely your God is a God
of gods and a Lord of kings and a revealer of mysteries,
since you have been able to reveal this mystery."

DANIEL 2:47

For nothing is hidden, except to be revealed;
nor has anything been secret, but that it would come to light.

MARK 4:22

4. Get other women in your corner.

Don't try to make it through this on your own. You've been
deeply hurt and need other women who can support, comfort
and pray with you. (It's important that your encouragers
aren't trying to pour more gasoline on the fire of your anger—
this will only make it worse!) Women who keep everything
bottled up inside are a volcano waiting to blow; putting off
asking for help adds more pressure to the coming explosion.

and our hope for you is firmly grounded,
knowing that as you are sharers of our sufferings,
so also you are sharers of our comfort.

2 CORINTHIANS 1:7

As most men who struggle with sexual sin think "I'm the
only one who struggles with this and can't tell others," so their
wives assume that "I can't tell anyone about this; no other
women talk about it so I must be alone." Remember, the surveys are showing that at least 50% of the men in the church
have a problem with porn or sex addiction. This means at least
50% of Christian women will at some point (when their husbands' struggle comes to light) have to deal with the pain of
their spouse's infidelity. You're not alone, and there are many
other women going through the same situation.

Some women avoid talking about their husbands' problem
because they're afraid others will think "she didn't do enough

of (fill in the blank with your insecurity of choice here) for him." Their husbands' sex addiction, they think, is condemning evidence there is some area in their marriage where they are deficient, and if other women find out they'll be judged. Always remember: your husband's sex addiction is not your fault. Satan's goal is to destroy your marriage, and he'll pour on the attack with thoughts of doubt, insecurity, and fear of judgment to keep you isolated and cut off from help and encouragement. (He uses this same method of attack on your husband to keep him from reaching out for help.)

You also need other women to avoid placing the full force of all your pain and anger on your husband alone. This isn't to say that you shouldn't express your feelings to him; you should, but remember, he's the source of your hurt. Sharing your grief and anger with other women is a safety valve that releases pressure from the marriage, which allows it to cool off and heal.

5. If you get a bad egg, drop it and look for a good one.

I hate to say this, but the truth is there are many Christians, pastors included, who aren't equipped or don't understand the issues going on with recovery from sexual sin. I receive emails from wives who were counseled by a pastor that "it's what men go through," "maybe you're not doing enough at home" (translation—giving him enough sex), or "you need to go home and submit to your husband." Advice like this is just as abusive as what your husband's doing to you.

If you reach out to the wrong person, don't allow this to discourage you into giving up and staying in isolation. Ask the Lord to lead you to someone who understands and can help.

We have women who serve the Blazing Grace ministry by emailing other wives for support, if you don't have someone there locally who you can talk to. Go to *www.blazinggrace.org* for more information.

6. Get in his corner.

Once your husband starts down the road to grace, don't expect him to become completely free for all time from all sexual sin overnight, especially if he's spent years saturating his mind with lust. (I'm not referring to sex outside of marriage here, which must stop immediately.) Most men get hooked on porn or sexual sin in their teen years, which means they're fighting a battle that's been a lifelong struggle. This is no easy task.

If your husband is showing you by consistent action that he wants to break free from sex addiction, join him in the fight. Pray with and for him every day, and ask other trusted friends to do the same. Ask him every week or two how he's doing with the battle (not daily); it will add more accountability into his life. His sex addiction is about medicating a hurting heart, and he's probably just as confused and scared as you are, in addition to being ashamed.

A man's wife can be his greatest asset in the battle against lust. You know his blind spots, weaknesses, and fears better than anyone else; your support means the most to him. If he goes on a business trip, for example, pray with him over the phone when he's in the hotel room, and ask him the next morning what he watched. When I travel and Michelle asks if I've kept the TV off, it lifts my spirit; she's showing me that she loves me in spite of my weaknesses, and is willing to fight with me. Satan wants you set against your husband, not standing with him in the battle.

Two are better than one because they
have a good return for their labor.
ECCLESIASTES 4:9

7. Don't look for comfort in the wrong places.

You may be tempted to find comfort in another man's arms, or get involved with other guys in chat rooms while your husband is floundering. Don't go there; it'll only add more stress, pain and pressure to a marriage that's already close to the breaking point. Don't watch porn movies to "find out where you are lacking," as Michelle did; this will just corrupt you and your family even more. Stand firm against the temptation to indulge in romantic fantasy, which is a setup for sexual sin. Keep your side of the street clean, regardless of what your husband's doing.

Some women have a tendency to turn to food for comfort during this time. Overeating won't solve the problem; like lust, it can put an emotional wall of shame between you, God, and your husband. Others try starving themselves to become the "perfect woman" so they can "fix their husband's problem." The perfect woman is a myth, and losing weight won't change his heart.

Seek comfort from other women, and, especially, with Jesus, Who is waiting for you to come to Him. If you don't have one already, get a journal and write your feelings out to the Lord, just as Job did in the midst of his sorrow. God can bless, comfort and speak to you through the outpouring of your heart; let Him love you.

Trust in Him at all times, O people;
Pour out your heart before Him; God is a refuge for us.
PSALMS 62:8

O may Your lovingkindness comfort me,
according to Your word to Your servant.
PSALMS 119:76

For just as the sufferings of Christ are ours
in abundance, so also our comfort is abundant through Christ.
2 CORINTHIANS 1:5

8. Seek healing for the deep wounds in your heart.
It's no accident that you married a man who's fallen into sexual sin. Often, the wife of a sex addict has married a man

who mirrors her father emotionally; women who were raised by emotionally absent fathers are often attracted to emotionally absent men. Many choose their spouses as a way to unwittingly resolve their childhood hurts, assuming that by changing their husband and/or creating "the perfect marriage and home," they'll resolve their pain.

Then, when their husband's betrayal cuts into these old sores of rejection and hurt, they find themselves slipping into deep depression, struggling with uncontrollable rage, or turning to counterfeit comforts. Just as your husband must deal with the root issues to completely remove the weed of his slavery to sexual sin, so you must face the core issues that feed your anger, insecurity, or depression. Leaving the roots of the deep, core wounds of your heart intact will keep you stuck in bitterness or depression long after your husband has recovered from his sex addiction, with the unwanted effect that the marriage can't move past his betrayal and heal.

Chapters seven through ten can help you look at these issues, as can the Prologue and Epilogue.

9. Make the Lord your First Love.

In her letter, Michelle wrote "I made you my everything," which is another way of saying I was an idol. After I confessed my adultery to her, I'll never forget when she said, "I had you up on a pedestal as this great Christian guy, and you've shattered it."

Men are not knights in shining armor, nor are we romantic dream machines who can fill up a woman's heart with all the love she craves; we're broken clay pots. As men (who are task orientated) can struggle with making work or ministry their god, women are prone to use their relationships as their primary source of self-esteem, acceptance, and love. When a woman makes her husband or family her god (i.e., "I am complete if I have the perfect husband with the perfect children"), she places unreasonable burdens and expectations on the backs of her loved ones. Then, when something goes wrong, like when she discovers her husband is a sinner who's addicted to porn and masturbation, her world collapses, taking the defective foundation her sense of self-worth was built on with it.

When the Lord first decided to give Eve to Adam in Genesis 2, He said, "It is not good for the man to be alone; I will make him a helper suitable for him." He did not intend that Adam be Eve's god, nor did he intend for Adam to worship her. You're not the answer to your husband's "question," just as he can't fill your heart with the love of God.

Our First Love should be Christ, not our spouse. It is in Him where we find completion, and the love that heals and fills empty hearts.

and in Him you have been made complete,
and He is the head over all rule and authority.

COLOSSIANS 2:10

For this reason I bow my knees before the Father, from whom
every family in heaven and on earth derives its name,
that He would grant you, according to the riches of His glory,
to be strengthened with power through His Spirit in the inner
man, so that Christ may dwell in your hearts through faith;
and that you, being rooted and grounded in love, may be able
to comprehend with all the saints what is the breadth and
length and height and depth, and to know the love of Christ
which surpasses knowledge, that you may be filled up
to all the fullness of God.

EPHESIANS 3:14–19

When a woman bases all of her self-esteem on whether her husband is sexually pure or not and goes on an all-out campaign to fix him, she's really saying that he's her god, and she's not loved unless he acts like one. God's love for you, my sister, isn't based on what your husband does, but on the fact that you are His daughter, created to enjoy the pleasure of a love relationship with Him.

…for in Him we live and move and exist, as even some of your own poets have said, 'For we also are His children.'

ACTS 17:28

for it is God who is at work in you,
both to will and to work for His good pleasure.

PHILLIPIANS 2:13

To rebuild your self-esteem on the solid rock of His love, examine the faulty foundation of lies that your life might be built on, and then replace it with the truth. I suggest that you spend some time with the Lord and ask Him to expose any false idols in your heart or wounds that need healing. You might also ask your husband and any other strong Christian lady friends what they see; the Lord often speaks through our closest friends.

When you've accepted God's love and He is first in your life, you can tell your husband to choose between you and porn, because your value comes from the Lord, not your husband. When God is first, if your husband struggles with lust your self-esteem won't take a big hit because you'll see your husband as a broken clay pot in need of grace, not the "everything" your life depends on. If God is first, you'll have an easier time getting dirty and coming along side your husband in the battle.

If you're struggling with accepting God's grace, I suggest that you read chapters 11–13.

10. Forgive your husband.
If you want to be completely healed from all the bitterness and pain of your husband's betrayal and you want your marriage to survive, at some point you will have to forgive him.

Forgiveness doesn't mean you try to short circuit the natural process of grieving, or attempt to stuff what happened. Forgiving your husband will be expensive; his debt, which he can never repay, will be completely erased.

Forgiving your husband for his sin against you may be the most Christ-like thing you do. Jesus allowed himself to be killed by people He loved so that they could be close to Him. You've been betrayed by the man you love; the only way you can remove every barrier between you and your husband is to forgive him.

Forgiveness doesn't give him permission to abuse your grace and indulge in sexual sin. It doesn't mean you stop holding him accountable for his actions, or that he no longer needs to go all out in the battle against lust.

Timing is important; don't cast your pearl of grace before a swine. If your husband is belligerently indulging in sexual sin, telling him that you forgive him will mean nothing to him; he'll trample it underfoot.

On the flip side, your gift of grace will be priceless to a broken man who wants his marriage restored. I'll never forget the night when Michelle forgave me; it was one of the most precious moments of our marriage. After writing her pardon in a letter, she read it to me one night. Her letter began by describing how I'd hurt her, something that was as painful for her to read as it was for me to hear. Then, in an amazing gift of grace for someone who'd hurt her so deeply, she read her forgiveness to me; we were both crying as we held each other in those moments. Immediately I had a sense that a wall that I had placed between us when I'd committed adultery had been lifted, and our emotional intimacy was restored.

If the time to forgive is ripe and you withhold it, your soul will remain poisoned with bitterness. The person who refrains from forgiving is always hurt more than the person who injured them. Your resentment will be a wall between you and your husband that will keep your marriage stuck in the past, thwarted by misfired communication, and writhing in pain.

Forgiveness is a powerful act of the will. It's not something you may feel like doing; if you wait until you do, it may never happen. To forgive is to choose to give up of all of your anger and release your husband from every expectation to make it right. When you release your husband, you're opening up a pipeline to your heart through which God's grace can flow and flush out all of your pain, anger, and sorrow.

Building a New Marriage

~

T he following are steps a husband and wife can take to rebuild their marriage from the wreckage of porn addiction or adultery. I'll address both sides, starting with the husband.

The big question after adultery has been committed is "do I tell my wife?" Both answers are fraught with problems. Keeping infidelity a secret doesn't change the fact that the marriage covenant has been shattered. On the other hand, confession is a journey into the unknown; no man can predict how his wife will respond when betrayal is revealed. She could immediately file for separation or divorce; if she agrees to stick it out the couple will be in for months of emotional strife and pain. Either way, there's no easy way out.

After I'd committed adultery and was pondering whether to tell Michelle, I asked John, who attended the same support group I did, for his advice. John had had many affairs, and I knew he'd gone through a rough time keeping his marriage together. I was hoping he would say "there's no way I'd tell her again," as I didn't want to confess to Michelle. But, his response rang in my ears. "You have to tell her or there will never be true intimacy in your marriage again; the woman you committed adultery with will always be between you and your wife."

The timing of such a revelation is important. If your wife has recently lost a parent, or if she's in counseling and dealing with trauma such as childhood sexual abuse or rape, confessing at the present moment is like taking a wrecking ball to a glass house. This doesn't mean she should never be told, only that you should wait.

As previously discussed in chapter seven, relationships are built on trust, and honesty is the cornerstone that sets the foundation. If you want your marriage to be pure and whole again, adultery must be confessed.

When you do, take 100% responsibility for your sin; don't add any barbs like, "if you were having more sex with me I wouldn't have been unfaithful." This is an abusive attempt to deflect blame on her.

Once disclosure has been made, expect an emotional roller coaster that could last a long time. When I asked John how long it took his wife to heal from his betrayal, his response was short and to the point. "Years."

My mouth dropped. "*Years???*" I asked in disbelief. "*Years???* I thought surely you were going to say a few weeks or maybe even months… but *years??!!*"

"Yes, years," John repeated firmly. "The old marriage you had is dead and you have to build a new one. This is going to take a lot of time and effort on your part; you've got to kill her with kindness and win her all over again."

Today, I know he was right; it was a number of years before Michelle's heart was restored.

Your consistent, determined efforts to stop all sexual sin give your wife a reason to trust again. If you're binging on porn and masturbation, or if you haven't broken off contact with the person you had an affair with, there's no reason she should stay with you; she has every right to ask for a separation until you get your priorities straight.

When she asks you for the details of "who, what, when and how often," answer truthfully and carefully. Avoid being overly graphic; your words create the scenes of a video she can play over and over in her mind. (Wives, before you start hitting him up for every detail, please see my comments below in your section.) Although your answers will cut her deeply, remember that honesty and truth provide healing and hope. Do not lie to her.

You *want* your wife to express her anger and hurt with you so she can process it; don't let her bottle up her feelings for a big explosion of rage. When she's angry, be quiet and listen, no matter what she says (swearing and insults included); don't attempt to defend what is your indefensible position. Remember, you hurt her. People who've been stabbed in the heart often scream in anguish; give her the freedom to express her pain. Love her and comfort her, when she lets you.

Respect her need for space, and don't push her if she needs time alone. If she withdraws from you for an extended period of time, *gently* coax her to open up; ask how she's feeling.

Give up your right to sex. This tells her that you care about her, and will help show her you're not the "it's all about me," guy you used to be. Tell your wife you realize the damage you've done, and that you'll back away from all expectation for sex until she's ready. You've raped your wife emotionally, and it will take time before she feels secure enough in the relationship for sexual intimacy. Crushed flowers need time to heal before they can open up and blossom again.

As soon as possible, start praying with your wife once a day, every day. At a Focus on the Family conference I attended, one of the speakers shared the following results of a survey on prayer in marriage: one out of two marriages end in divorce when a husband and wife don't pray together, of those who pray on a consistent basis, one out of 1,000 divorce. You need the Lord's involvement in your marriage as quickly as possible so He can bind you together again. Confess your sins to Him with your wife; ask Him to heal her, and cleanse your marriage of all evil. She can pray for the Lord's healing, protection, and guidance in your life. Ask for specific prayer requests from each other every night.

As the spiritual leader of your marriage, the responsibility of instigating prayer with your wife lies on your shoulders. Regardless of how you may feel after recent events, I encourage you to press forward in making daily prayer with your wife a permanent part of your marriage.

And if one can overpower him who is alone, two can resist him.
A cord of three strands is not quickly torn apart.

ECCLESIASTES 4:12

For the husband is the head of the wife, as Christ also is the
head of the church, He Himself being the Savior of the body.

EPHESIANS 5:23

The old marriage is dead and you need to build a new one; get back to the basics, which is to be your wife's best friend. Court her all over again; date her—with no expectation for sex. Open up your heart to her and let her get to know you; share your fears, hurts, and joys. Listen to her. Do the things she likes that you've probably neglected, such as opening the door, bringing her flowers, calling her from the office during the day, leaving her a card in the morning, or giving her a small gift. (Note: do not try to "buy her friendship" by giving her an expensive trinket—she'll see through this immediately!) Pour the ointment of grace and love on her and let her see by your actions that she's precious to you.

> *Love is patient, love is kind and is not jealous;*
> *love does not brag and is not arrogant, does not act*
> *unbecomingly; it does not seek its own, is not provoked,*
> *does not take into account a wrong suffered, does not rejoice in*
> *unrighteousness, but rejoices with the truth; bears all things,*
> *believes all things, hopes all things, endures all things.*

1 CORINTHIANS 13:4–7

> *Husbands, love your wives, just as Christ also loved the church*
> *and gave Himself up for her…*

EPHESIANS 5:25

Remember the Lord's simple instruction on how to make a marriage work: "Husbands love your wives." Not, "husbands preach to, manipulate, fix, or control." Work at accepting and loving her as she is and letting the Lord take care of her defects. Marriages get messy when either spouse starts trying to fix the other; surrender her weaknesses into His hands.

If the two of you are having a hard time communicating without fighting, get marital counseling from an experienced Christian counselor or pastor ASAP. Ask them if they've had experience helping couples heal from adultery; if not, keep looking until you find one. Marital counseling can be a safe way to work through sensitive issues that may be too emotionally charged for the two of you to face alone.

When a marriage is cracked wide open by a traumatic event like adultery, unhealthy communication and relational patterns such as dependency, power and control issues, spousal worship, and inappropriate boundaries are often exposed. In the process of facing and dealing with these issues in a healthy way, you will rebuild a new, stronger marriage. Again, if you find yourselves getting overwhelmed in trying to juggle your wife's pain, your recovery and rebuilding the marriage, seek help from a Christian marital counselor.

The Lord should be your first love and priority, not your wife. When He is the primary source of your life, love, and acceptance, you won't try to make your wife (or sex) fill needs she wasn't meant to. She'll trust and respect a broken man of integrity who's committed to following the Lord over all others far more than a guy who's still trying to fake it and do everything by his strength.

Ask those in your support group to hold you and your wife in prayer often. I've seen the Lord bring marriages back from the dead, even after the wife had told the husband she'd wanted a divorce. Prayer plays an enormous role in the healing process; the more people praying for you and your wife, the better.

Now we turn to the spouse.

Adultery is a deeply painful, traumatic event to recover from; your emotional state may bounce between a state of shock, blistering anger, and tears of grief. This is a normal response to betrayal by a loved one. Remember, his adultery is not your fault. Your spouse's choice to sin against you was his alone; never accept the blame for it from him, or anyone else.

You have the right to ask your spouse for every detail of his sin. However, consider that knowing the color of the other person's hair, or what your spouse did with them sexually will add vivid color to a video you can torture yourself with repeatedly. You should ask how long an affair took place, how often and with what person(s), but grilling him for every intrinsic, gory detail will probably do more damage than good. Consider what you should ask, as well as what you shouldn't; what's healthy and needed to rebuild trust versus what will be abusive to you. Wounds need to be cleaned out, not rubbed with salt or cut deeper.

Work to release pressure in the marriage by sharing what you're going through with at least one other lady outside of the marriage. If you don't have a friend like this at present, ask the Lord to provide you with a person, group or counselor to turn to.

Be very careful about who you share with—especially when it comes to family. Telling Aunt Betty the Battle Axe who has it in for your husband is a big mistake. Instead of serving as a conduit for healing, persons like this will pour gasoline on the fire of your anger and sabotage the healing process. Telling family, at least in the beginning, isn't often a good idea. You don't need your relatives adding pressure to the cooker by pushing you to divorce your husband every time they see you. Worse, some family members blame the wife when a husband falls into adultery with statements like "Oh Dearie, it's all in your head; you just need to live up to your wifely duties." (Laurie Hall described the hell of telling the wrong persons in her book *An Affair of the Mind*.) Proceed carefully and probe the person you might talk to for their attitudes about adultery, brokenness and grace before opening up with them.

Hold your husband accountable, but don't try to work his recovery for him. Give him the space and grace to stumble, learn, and discover on his own. Let the Lord be His God. Be his wife and best friend, not his mother.

Your husband's decision to cut lust out of his life may force you to look at some purity issues of your own. Magazines like People (which is often packed with pictures of scantily clad women and filled with juicy gossip), or lingerie catalogs like Victoria's Secret will be a stumbling block for him. They also promote a lifestyle and message that is subtly corrupting to you and your children.

When a couple begins the process of rebuilding their life, the wife sometimes finds she has some compromise in her life. Most of the programs on television today have a spiritually numbing effect at best; many are outright evil. I often hear men complain that their wives are watching programs, buying magazines or reading books that are sexually explicit. (A romance novel that glorifies adultery or fornication is porn, just as the X–rated content your husband used to watch.) Your commitment to live a pure life before God should be just as sure as your husband's. If he wants to shut off all cable or TV service to your home, support him. Allow him to be the spiritual leader you've wanted him to be.

I will set no worthless thing before my eyes; I hate the work of those who fall away; It shall not fasten its grip on me.

PSALMS 101:3

Finally, brethren, whatever is true, whatever is honorable, whatever is right, whatever is pure, whatever is lovely, whatever is of good repute, if there is any excellence and if anything worthy of praise, dwell on these things. The things you have learned and received and heard and seen in me, practice these things, and the God of peace will be with you.

PHILLIPPIANS 4:8–9

Your husband is a broken man; a sinner. Women who base their self-esteem on their husband's recovery are setting themselves up for a painful fall, because any attempt to fix him will ultimately end in disaster. Sparks fly and marriages get messy when an insecure wife makes her husband's recovery her god; she loses her identity and dignity in an altar of enmeshment.

When both spouses make the Lord their first source of love, the marriage can become what God designed it to be: one man and one woman who are best friends for life. Grace flows freely through a union that isn't clogged up with unrealistic expectations; be determined to make Christ your First Love.

When you're ready to forgive your husband, I suggest you write your pardon out in a letter and read it to him. In the first part of your letter, describe how his unfaithfulness affected you. Take your time and express your hurt and anguish to him; describe what you both have lost. Then, finish your letter by forgiving him of his sin against you.

Schedule at least an hour during a quiet time of the day when you know there will be no distractions to read your letter to your husband. Take the phone off the hook, and consider sending the kids to Grandma's for one night. This may one of the most tender, sacred and intimate moments of your marriage, and you don't want interruptions.

Take your time, and minister to each other after you read your letter. Cry over what was lost, and rejoice at the new life your marriage has been given. Afterwards, I suggest that both of you pray; ask the Lord to complete the process of cleansing your marriage and healing both of you of all pain, bitterness, and sin.

May the Lord bless both of you.
May He purify and cleanse your family.
May His healing grace and peace abound
to you in fullest measure.
May He make your marriage fruitful in love.
May your marriage glorify Him.

appendix c

Recommended Reading

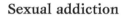

Sexual addiction

Breaking Free: Understanding Sexual Addiction and the Healing Power of Jesus, by Russ Willingham.

Written by a Christian counselor who had his own struggle with lust, Willingham goes deep into the root causes of sexual addiction and then points the reader to Jesus.

For Wives

An Affair of the Mind, by Laurie Hall.

This book had a profound effect in showing me the damage I was causing to my family. I recommend it for men as well as wives.

Living with Your Husband's Secret Wars, by Marsha Means.

Great advice on how a wife can cope with her husband's sex addiction.

For Couples

I Surrender All: Rebuilding a Marriage Broken by Pornography, by Clay and Renee Crosse.

Clay and Renee describe the healing process they went through in their marriage from Clay's struggle with porn addiction.

Other:

The Pursuit of God; The Human Thirst for the Divine, by AW Tozer.

Few books stoke the flames of desire to seek the Living God as well as this one.

Anything by Oswald Chambers.

I read *My Utmost for His Highest* every day. Chambers has a way of cutting to the heart of what our relationship with Christ should be about—Him, not ministry, "doing for God," or religion.

So You Want to Be Like Christ? Eight Essentials to Get You There, by Chuck Swindoll.

An excellent book on deepening our walk with the Lord.

The Ragamuffin Gospel, by Brennan Manning.
Manning's classic treatise on grace.

Rich Mullins, An Arrow Pointing to Heaven, by James Bryan Smith.

Rich used to sign autographs with "Be God's," as opposed to "Be good," which he sometimes felt the church focused too much on. Called a "Devotional Biography" by the author, this book provides a fresh look at the love of God through the life of Rich Mullins.

Notes

Chapter 1

1. blogs.christianpost.com/bright-ideas/infographic-porn-addiction-in-america-19411/ December 30, 2013
2. The Inquisitr, December 26, 2013
3. Gen-XXX-Teens-Addicted-in-a-World-Awash-in-Porn. www.cbn.com/cbn-news/us/2012/November/Gen-XXX-Teens-Addicted-in-a-World-Awash-in-Porn/CBN News, December 3, 2012.
4. www.business-standard.com/article/news-ani/more-people-hooked-to-porn-in-uk-than-social-networks-113072700414_1.html. The Business Standard, July 27, 2013.
5. blogs.christianpost.com/guest-views/sexual-sin-in-the-ministry-8613/. The Christian Post, March 8, 2012.
6. archive.news10.net/news/national/245195/5/Survey-Kids-access-porn-sites-at-6-start-flirting-online-at-8. ABC News, May 15, 2013.
7. www.iol.co.za/lifestyle/family/kids/children-as-young-as-11-watch-porn-1.1572232. IOL Lifestyle, September 3, 2013.
8. Gen-XXX-Teens-Addicted-in-a-World-Awash-in-Porn. www.cbn.com/cbn-news/us/2012/November/Gen-XXX-Teens-Addicted-in-a-World-Awash-in-Porn/CBN News, December 3, 2012.
9. Gen-XXX-Teens-Addicted-in-a-World-Awash-in-Porn. www.cbn.com/cbn-news/us/2012/November/Gen-XXX-Teens-Addicted-in-a-World-Awash-in-Porn/CBN News, December 3, 2012.
10. churchm.ag/porn-stats/ as quoted from a pastormark.tv survey, March 27, 2012
11. blogs.christianpost.com/bright-ideas/infographic-porn-addiction-in-america-19411/ December 30, 2013

Chapter 2

1. Ted Roberts, *Pure Desire* (Ventura, California: Regal Books, 1999), page 45.
2. Excerpt taken from Laurie Hall's book *An Affair of the Mind*, a Focus on the Family book. Copyright©1996, Laurie Hall. All rights reserved. International copyright secured. Used by permission. Page 149
3. Ibid, page 149

Chapter 3

1. Taken from *My Utmost for His Highest* by Oswald Chambers, edited by James Reimann, ©1992 by Oswald Chambers Publications Assn., Ltd., and used by permission of Discovery House Publishers, Grand Rapids MI 49501. All rights reserved. From the April 10th reading.
2. www.divorcewizards.com: "Porn Matters—Divorce and Pornography Statistics."
3. The statistics for single parent families came from Crown Financial Ministries' website: *www.crown.org/FinancialWisdom/church/single_parent/statistics.asp#Fatherless and fathermag.com: www.fathermag.com/news/2756–suicide.shtml.*
4. Ibid, from the above sources
5. Ibid, from the above sources
6. Ibid, from the above sources
7. Ibid, from the above sources
8. Ibid, from the above sources

Chapter 4

1. Taken from *My Utmost for His Highest* by Oswald Chambers, edited by James Reimann, ©1992 by Oswald Chambers Publications Assn., Ltd., and used by permission of Discovery House Publishers, Grand Rapids MI 49501. All rights reserved. From the December 1st reading.

Chapter 6

1. JRR Tolkien, *The Fellowship of the Ring* (Boston, New York: Houghton Mifflin Company, ©1954, 1965, 1966 by JRR Tolkien), page 54.
2. *The Return of the King*, directed by Peter Jackson (New Line Cinema, 2003).
3. JRR Tolkien, *The Silmarillion, Second Edition* (Boston, New York: Houghton Mifflin Company, 2001), pages 287–288.
4. Dr. Archibald Hart, *The Sexual Man* (Dallas: Word Publishing, 1994), pages 136–139.
5. Excerpt taken from Laurie Hall's book *An Affair of the Mind*, a Focus on the Family book. Copyright©1996, Laurie Hall. All rights reserved. International copyright secured. Used by permission. Pages 105 and 106 from her chapter "Let Me Entertain Me." Laurie's treatment of masturbation is one of the best I've ever read. Perhaps few men have written so clearly on the topic because they don't want to face the idea that they can live without self-sex, and they don't see their self and sex absorption as clearly as their wives do.

Chapter 7

1. Shelley Lubben, "The Truth Behind the Fantasy of Porn." *www.shelleylubben.com.*
2. Eva Marie Everson, *Sex, Lies and the Media,* (Colorado Springs, CO: Cook Communications, 2005), page 158.

Chapter 8

1. David Seamands, *Healing for Damaged Emotions* (Wheaton, Illinois: Victor Books, Division of Scripture Press Publications, 1981), page 29.
2. Although this quote is widely attributed to GK Chesterton, the American Chesterton Society (www.chesterton.org) reported that it was Bruce Marshall who originally penned it in his 1945 book *The World, the Flesh and Father Smith* (published by Houghton Mifflin Co., New York).

NOTES

Chapter 9

1. Thomas Kincade, *My Father's World* (Nashville: Thomas Nelson Publishers, 2000), page 85.
2. www.momscape.com/articles/father-quotes.htm.
3. Thomas Kincade, *My Father's World* (Nashville: Thomas Nelson Publishers, 2000), page 57.
4. www.momscape.com/articles/father-quotes.htm.
5. Reprinted by permission. *Wild at Heart* by John Eldredge, 2001, Thomas Nelson Inc., Nashville, Tennessee, page 62. All rights reserved.
6. Gary Smalley and John Trest, *The Blessing* (Nashville: Thomas Nelson Publishers, 1986), pages 24–29.
7. From Ross Campbell's book *How to Really Love Your Child* (Wheaton, Illinois: Victor Books, 1977), page 73, as quoted in Smalley and Trent's, *The Blessing* (Nashville: Thomas Nelson Publishers, 1986), page 44.
8. Other stories in Scripture of men who were affected by their father's passive leadership include Eli's two sons, who slept with the women who served at the tent of meeting (2 Samuel 2–3), and David's kids (see 1 Kings 1:5–6). Amnon raped Tamar, and then was killed by Absalom, who later led the nation of Israel in the civil war that cost him his life. David didn't rebuke Amnon for raping Tamar, or Absalom for killing Amnon.
9. Reprinted by permission. *Wild at Heart* by John Eldredge, 2001, Thomas Nelson Inc., Nashville, Tennessee, page 71. All rights reserved.
10. Used by permission. B&H Publishing Group, Nashville, TN. Excerpts taken from the book *Rich Mullins, An Arrow Pointing to Heaven*, B&H Publishing Group, © 2002, page xii.
11. *Dad*, directed by Gary David Goldberg, (Universal Studios, 1989).
12. H. Norman Wright, *Always Daddy's Little Girl* (Ventura, CA: Regal Books), pages 11–12.
13. Used by permission. B&H Publishing Group, Nashville, TN. Excerpts taken from the book *Rich Mullins, An Arrow Pointing to Heaven*, B&H Publishing Group, © 2002, pages xii–xiii.

Chapter 10

1. Russell Willingham, *Breaking Free* (Downer's Grove, Illinois: Intervarsity Press, 1999), page 131.
2. James Bryan Smith, *Rich Mullins, An Arrow Pointing to Heaven* (Nashville: Broadman and Holman Publishers, 2000), page xii.

Chapter 11

1. Calculated by using $35.00 an ounce for silver, $1,500.00 an ounce for gold.

Chapter 12

1. Taken from *My Utmost for His Highest* by Oswald Chambers, edited by James Reimann, ©1992 by Oswald Chambers Publications Assn., Ltd., and used by permission of Discovery House Publishers, Grand Rapids MI 49501. All rights reserved. From the June 11th reading.
2. Charles Swindoll, *So You Want to Be Like Christ?* (Nashville, W Publishing Group, div. of Thomas Nelson Publishers, 2005), page 40.
3. AW Tozer, *The Pursuit of God; The Human Thirst for the Divine* (Camp Hill, PA: 1982), page 9.
4. AW Tozer, *The Pursuit of God; The Human Thirst for the Divine* (Camp Hill, PA: 1982), page 18.

Chapter 13

1. *Les Miserables*, directed by Billie August, (Sony Pictures, 1998).

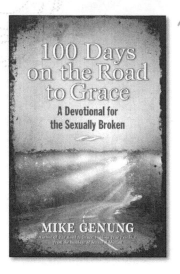

100 Days on the Road to Grace, a Devotional for the Sexually Broken, offers a collection of 100 powerful readings that expand on Mike Genung's first book.

Topics include:

- ✦ The path to freedom from porn and sexual addiction.
- ✦ Keys to rebuilding your character.
- ✦ Coping with emotions such as anger, depression, and fear.
- ✦ Rebuilding trust and bringing healing to your marriage and family.
- ✦ Bitterness and forgiveness.
- ✦ Breaking the bondage of self.
- ✦ Spiritual Warfare.
- ✦ Revitalizing the relationship with God.
- ✦ Living a life that counts for eternity

And many more.

If you're hungry for God and want more than just freedom from sexual sin, this book is for you. Available at:

www.RoadToGrace.net

Mike Genung can be reached at:

BLAZING GRACE PUBLISHING
PO Box 25763
Colorado Springs, CO 80936

www.roadtograce.net

⤬

See *www.roadtograce.net* and *blazinggrace.org*
for more articles and information on future books,
including *The Road to Grace Devotional*.

To Order More Copies of This Book

Mail this form to:
BLAZING GRACE PUBLISHING
PO Box 25763
Colorado Springs, CO 80936

Company Name: _____

Name: _____

Address: _____

City:_____ State:_____ Zip: _____

Country: _____

Phone:_____ Email:_____

A phone number is required for Express Mail and shipments outside of the United States. Please provide a phone number or email address in the event we need to contact you.

Please send me _____ copies of The Road to Grace at US$14.95 each.

To obtain the correct postage rate for your area, please go to
postcalc.usps.gov/ and obtain a quote. We ship by Media Mail
(in the U.S.), Priority Mail and Express Mail Service.
Enter a shipping weight of 1 pound for each book you want to order.

Total books _____ X $14.95 = $_____

Shipping cost: $_____

Method:_____

Colorado Residents please add 7.4% Sales Tax: $_____

Total amount: $_____

Please make checks out to Blazing Grace Publishing.